Breaking the silence on child abuse

First printed 2018

ISBN 978-1-84625-606-6

British Library Cataloguing in Publication Data available

Published by Day One Publications
Ryelands Road, Leominster, HR6 8NZ
☎ 01568 613 740 FAX 01568 611 473
email—sales@dayone.co.uk
web site—www.dayone.co.uk

Original cover design by Benjamin Hughes
Cover illustration by Kathryn Chedgzoy
Printed by TJ International

This book is dedicated to my wife and to my
fellow survivors who know the heaven and hell
of living the new life. It is also dedicated to all
the supporters who, like Sue, stand by survivors
with the compassion of Jesus. You are my heroes
and heroines and heaven's too!

Endorsements

'The shocking news headlines of child abuse have brought a long-silenced subject into every home. Frankly, yet sensitively, written, Robert's personal story is far more than simply a retelling of the tragedy. It is a thoughtful, practical, and deeply pastoral response to a cruel practice perpetrated on innocent children. Firmly rooted in Biblical counselling, there are no quick-fix or glib answers, but the value of essential information and advice. Every pastor and elder should read it — who knows how many 'survivors' there may be in our congregations unknown even to the leaders? Certainly, all who have been abused, or are caring for those who have been emotionally damaged, will find great wisdom and help in this small but valuable book. I warmly recommend it to those who are, or may be, involved in such care. The subject is widespread and life-damaging, and we need to be equipped to care—*Breaking the Silence* will unquestionably assist in that.

Brian H Edwards, author, pastor for thirty years, Chairman of Christian Prison Resourcing.

'Breaking the Silence was a tough read, but really worth working through. The horror of reading how human beings could inflict such pain and anguish on a small boy was shocking. It also uncovered areas of the abuse I suffered as a child. Following counselling, I thought I had it all 'sorted', but this book brought to light unperceived issues and how to deal with them. I found it enormously helpful and had a number of 'light bulb' moments during the read. Great thanks to Robert for his openness and showing that there is a way from victim, to survivor and ultimately thriver.'

Noëlle, a happy and grateful thriver

'A brave and biblical account of one believer's journey from early sexual abuse to ongoing Christian ministry. Robert's book bears all the marks of authenticity including the long suffering such experiences produce and the hard-won wisdom of a life spent seeking to live for God.'

Peter Lewis, Senior Pastor, Cornerstone Church, Nottingham

'This book traces the journey of one man from the depths of despair after experiencing abuse, to an emergence into the Light of Life. It describes honestly the journey of faith in God which tells us much about how we all experience the puzzle of working out our faith in fear and trembling.

Robert brings us to understand much about the depths of his faith, which he and I would gladly recommend to all.'

Chris Whiteley, General Secretary Old Baptist Union

'In my work as a paediatrician I see children who have suffered the horrors of sexual abuse. I witness the short-term havoc it can wreak in individuals and families. Our energies focus, rightly so, on preventing the abuse happening in the first place. But what about those who aren't so fortunate? Is there really any hope for the abused? Or is it a case of 'move on and let time be the healer?' As reports of historic child abuse continue to explode around us, Robert's account (including the powerful chapter giving his wife's perspective) honestly and vulnerably portrays the long-term effects of this tragedy, truly 'breaking the silence'. In that sense, it is a difficult read. And yet hope courses through these pages. Therapists can and do help. But the key message hits home—there is only one Doctor of a broken heart, only one who offers true and lasting freedom from the secret shame carried by so many today.'

Dr John Greenall, National Field Director of the Christian Medical Fellowship and a Paediatrician in Bedfordshire.

Child sexual abuse is a subject that concerns far more people than has been realized until recently, and which can have tragic long-term consequences. Many will find it liberating and helpful to read the book, even if only to know they are not alone. Robert has thought through the issues and his own experience to move beyond the damaging effects. Many of the spiritual remedies suggested are generic for other forms of depression. The author also shows that a wide range of strategies may be needed to meet the various causes and aftermath of different people's experience.

Mike Plant, Former General Secretary of the Evangelical Fellowship of Congregational Churches

This is a remarkable book, written with courage, openness and honesty. It traces the history of the tremendous struggle that the author, and indeed his wife, went through in seeking recovery from the defiling and traumatic experience of physical and sexual abuse he suffered as a child, and the biblical way out of such a black hole. It deserves to be read by many, especially those who have suffered such abuse, as well as Christian workers who have to try to minister to such sufferers. However, some may need to read it with care: some who have been abused, when converted, are transformed relatively quickly and are able to put the past behind them more easily than others; others who are more sensitive, may find that it introduces complications into their thinking that were not there before. Counsellors should be careful to whom they recommend the book. Nevertheless it is an extraordinary account and could be used greatly to help both survivors and counsellors. The Reference list of other books is also very useful. Warmly recommended.

Dr Stanley Jebb, Minister (retired), Bible College Lecturer and Author

'This is a refreshingly honest and courageous look at the journey from being a victim of abuse, to being a survivor and then a thriver. Robert draws on both his own experience and the work of others as he describes this journey. This book combines the reality of pain with hope, based on faith in God'.

Dr Debbie Hawker, Clinical Psychologist, college lecturer and Chair of Care Forum Global Connections.

The author has over thirty years pastoral experience in four different churches. He was a teacher for fifteen years and now works with men in different settings, inside and outside prison. He has been married to Sue for forty years, has five children and seven grandchildren.

'God has taken his place in the divine counsel; in
the midst of the gods he holds judgment:
How long will you judge unjustly and show
partiality to the wicked?
Give justice to the weak and the fatherless;
maintain the right of the afflicted and destitute.
Rescue the weak and the needy; deliver them
from the hand of the wicked.'
Psalm 82:1–4

Contents

Acknowledgements

Writing this book has been both a painful and a greatly blessed journey and still is. But I thank God it has been written with the support and involvement of many people. It is to these dear ones who I want to give my heart felt thanks.

There are many who have offered their comments after reading a manuscript. Anne, Noelle, Peter, John, Stanley, Mike, Chris and Glenn, are some of these. Thank you to each one of you and those who have then given their endorsement to the book.

A special thanks goes to the survivors who have shared the pain and healing of their journeys with us. Marilyn, Jonathan, and Alice, whose real names have been replaced in the book, are just a few.

I owe a great debt to David Fortune who has patiently given his advice on numerous draft copies. It has been the editing skills of Brian Edwards that have shaped the final version. His insights and suggestions have been invaluable. Both these brothers caught the vision and saw the potential of this journey for survivors. Without their support and encouragement I don't think that it would have gone to print in this format. I would also like to thank Mark Roberts and his team at Day One Christian Ministries, for their untiring efforts and professionalism in meeting a tight deadline.

Benjamin Hughes always produces artwork of a high standard and I am grateful to him for this book jacket and all his designs for the Courageous Exchange Programme.

You don't often have a chance to name some of your heroes so here we go: Samual Rutherford, Robert M McCheyne, Jim & Elizabeth Elliot, Richard Sibbs, C H Spurgeon, Martin Loyd Jones, Bishop J C Ryle, Arthur Pink, Wayne Grudem, Jim Packer, John Piper, John MacArthur, Peter Lewis, Stanley Jebb and more have all left their mark.

Lastly, I want to say a big thank you to all our friends and family who have been an influence for great good in my life, too many to mention, but Ken and Michael you are wonderfully faithful. But the biggest thanks must go to those who have journeyed closely and experienced the greatest pain. My family, particularly my parents, one of my brothers, the wider family and, of course, most of all my dear wife and our children who have often unknowing been an influence. Your kindnesses and encouragement have kept me going.

Sincere love and gratitude to each one of you.

Robert

Introduction

Before we start, let me warn you that this is not an interesting story to read and put on the shelf. It's a story of real life with its ups and downs, complexities, joy and pain. I describe my journey away from the impact of child abuse to the present-day freedom. It is an unpleasant story but at the same time it breathes hope and recovery for survivors. I have chosen to take the lid off this tragedy so that hope can grow and the issue can be seen for what it really is. Like no other time in history, society is being shaken by the size of this issue provoking questions like: What is it like to live with the secret of an abused childhood? How can a survivor restore their life? What can the church do to help?

There is a journey of transformation, and by telling my story I hope that survivors will be encouraged to take their own journey. It is only right that survivors have access to this hope and, given time, the gradual but real and positive changes can take place. My prayer is that victims become survivors and that survivors become thrivers. But it is also my prayer that Christians will grow in their understanding and appreciation of courageous survivors who live each day with the trauma of their past. Most survivors don't need helping in the way we often see 'help' (they are amazingly resourceful individuals), but they do need support. A support which is appropriate and relevant. Therefore, I am also writing for those who could support survivors.

Now that the lid has come off the whole scandal of child abuse, what are we to do with it all? What can be done to restore priceless lives? I am convinced that the Body of Jesus (the Christian church) has the resources, the call and the capacity. It has stepped up to the mark in the past, and pioneered major developments in our society and across the world. The challenge today is to understand the impact of this trauma on individuals so that we can pioneer once again. Christians are being called today to handle this tragedy in a way that breathes hope and gives support to people who, much of the time, have little idea of how God sees them. We need answers to tough questions and answers that lead to the right actions.

I come from a creative background and later trained to be a pastor. This might explain why the style of this book moves from the expressive to the Scriptures and then back again.

You may like to know that there is a workbook that can be used with this book. Group work is a way forward for some, while others prefer to look into these things by themselves. The workbook is designed to help progress on a journey of recovery. (*Breaking the Silence on Child Abuse—A Study* by Robert Lightowler, Day One Publishers, 2018)

This book and the workbook are part of the Courageous Exchange Programme.

Section 1
Abused—The childhood trauma

'Keep looking below surface appearances. Don't shrink from doing so just because you might not like what you find.'

Colin Powel, Chairman of the US Joint Chiefs of Staff (1989–93)

'There is nothing concealed that will not be disclosed, or hidden that will not be made known.'

Jesus Christ, Luke 12:2

Chapter 1

A heinous crime

> 'The survivor is left with fundamental problems in basic trust, autonomy, and initiative ... The survivor's intimate relationships are driven by the hunger for protection and care and are haunted by the fear of abandonment or exploitation.'
>
> Judith Herman[I]

It was another night wrestling with sleeplessness. Eventually, when I did go to sleep in the early hours, I dreamt that I was conducting a school orchestra. Most of the students were late for a rehearsal and so, to fill time, I told them a story from my past. I was being open about an experience at boarding school and it was clearly reaching their hearts. When I woke up, it dawned on me that I must bring into the open things that happened to me when I was a child.

Insurmountable challenges that I had faced for many years, kept resurfacing and demanded to be spoken about. I needed to be open with the ones closest to me about the secret pain. To many people I may have appeared to be a successful schoolteacher or a kind church leader, yet behind the face of respectability was a dark secret. I have a lovely wife and five beautiful children (and now seven, just as beautiful, grandchildren). Shortly after waking up, I told Sue about some of the details. I've never seen her cry so much as we sat in the bedroom deep in one another's arms. Something was happening, and we knew that this was a new day after decades of darkness. A heinous crime had been committed; an evil in its destructive force which left a wound, an unseen disability. Now was the time for surgery. Now was the unexpected time for a gradual journey of healing. A new day had dawned.

My story in brief, is this. At ten years old, I was sexually abused by two teachers at boarding school and physically abused by two others. Severe beatings were quite normal. The head teacher took the lead using a variety of implements to inflict maximum pain. But it was another teacher, usually at night, who took it to a higher, sadistic level. This went on for three years. Later, as a teenager, I experimented with drugs and had a couple of near overdose experiences. I used alcohol and fantasy to escape the pain.

The gift I had as a child was that I could sing. Therefore, my dear dad, on the recommendation of our church organist, took me to voice trials for entry into a cathedral choir. The first voice trial was at St John's College, Cambridge and I remember being bought an ice cream when I was not accepted. We went to another cathedral where, after the voice trial, I passed. The choirmaster led me from the crypt, where the choristers would practice, into the nave. He asked me to sing a high note and, to my amazement, the echoes danced around the expanse of this vast building. I felt then as an eight-year-old boy I had the voice of an angel which would somehow please God my Father. Oh, there was such ecstatic delight in singing.

It was just before my ninth birthday that I moved away from my parents and three brothers living in Bradford to the boarding school. The rugged Yorkshire accent was soon replaced with syrupy-smooth refined tones. Homesickness, common among new boys, was subdued by adventure, hard work and the disciplines of the school's routines. The next three years were to be filled with the greatest of joys, but also with horrendous encounters.

Singing in harmony or solo in such a majestic building in front of large audiences or at times with an orchestra, was truly exhilarating— a 'magical' experience. We were taken on special outings such as to an airforce base or to a concert. There was the rolling countryside where we walked, the midnight feasts or the ghost stories, playing in an orchestra, scouting activities and sleeping out in a tent. Even times of illness in the sickbay were quite enjoyable! There were the things I did not do particularly well, but I enjoyed them because they were 'manly': boxing, rugby, cricket and cross-country runs in the snow.

Tucked into these rich and colourful experiences were the dark and deathly moments with the masters. At the time, they seemed to be part of the routine of boarding school life. I accepted that the punishments were necessary, but struggled with the extent to which they were taken. Getting a 'good thrashing' happened quite regularly. It could be for something as simple as asking to leave class to go to the toilet, or for not divulging who was talking in the dormitory after lights out.

One occasion stands out as completely unjust in my young mind. I had run away after an evening service, but when it got dark, I gave in and knocked on the door of the only house in sight. I remember it as if it were yesterday. The husband was building a model of the commercial plane he flew. The couple kindly phoned my dad instead of the school and he drove many miles from home to collect me. When he returned me to the school, he did what I asked him to do. He requested the headteacher to agree that on this occasion I would not be caned. Yet as soon as my father had left, I was given the traditional 'six-of-the-best.' What everyone knows who has suffered it, it is six of the worst! Once, as I was trying to get away from a beating I ran around the head teacher's desk knocking his telephone to the floor. I thought, at the time, that most of the boys were punished in this excessive way. It seemed normal to be overpowered and humiliated. When I objected to the injustice of it, I was thrashed even more.

Then there were the emotional games and sexual exploitation. I was lonely, so I welcomed the attention some masters gave, even though I knew it was wrong. The confusion was that this was a place of achievement and development. Boys were passing their exams and moving up to famous public schools. It was also a place where I felt secure. This was my new family. But it was here that adults crossed a line to become no more than common thieves. There were three masters who picked on me. One housemaster got his pleasure from punishing sadistically, while another from regarding me, I guess, as his boyfriend. And to another—that I remember most distinctly—I was just his plaything.

I kept all these events a secret for over thirty years because of the shame. Eventually I spoke to the police. However, what troubled me was that I could only remember some things that one teacher persuaded me to do to him. The police interviewed him but he denied everything. It was an ongoing relationship with the assistant choir master that was almost completely wiped from my memory. Yet I know he had molested me repeatedly. Amnesia is common in some victims. I can remember visiting his room so that he could help me with a piece of music that I was composing. We would work at the harpsichord and sit on his bed. He eventually allowed me to play the piece after an evening service on the mighty three manual organ in the cathedral.

Something happened on those visits to his room when we were alone.

My mind used to have such a firm grasp on our mutual sexual activities that a piece of news he gave me was shocking. Just before I left the cathedral at the age of thirteen, he took me aside to tell me that he was engaged to be married. I remember my reaction caused him to panic. We were in public and I asked him, rather too loudly, how a man like him could possibly get married to a woman. After I had left the cathedral, he drove across to a town near Wigan in Lancashire, where my family now lived, to see me. He took me for a drive, supposedly to enjoy his new sports car. We stopped in the countryside and he took me into the trees. He wanted me to handle him but I politely but firmly refused. He drove me home and that, thankfully, was the last time I saw him.

There, I have said it! I'm sorry if you find this upsetting—really sorry. Although this happened fifty years ago, at this time of writing it still causes a fear to rise in me, a shame and an anger. I want to cry, but I will not.

While in contact with the police I discovered that not all the boys were being sexually abused. What I thought at the time was normal for an all-male environment was not true. I was in my forties when I discovered this and it tormented me because it seemed that I was singled out. Then at the age of sixty-three I heard that others had come forward. I was not the only one after all.

In the last few years I have been able to speak about it to my family. I have been an active member of a church for most of my life and a church leader, but nobody until recently, apart from my wife, knew about my past. Now I enjoy something of a new freedom because of the journey God is taking me on to bind up my broken heart.

‘ Life stinks!

‘God is great enough to bear our anger. He can absorb its full impact. It is safe to spend our anger against His bosom until, in the quiet, he lets us feel the pulse of His own broken heart.’[1]

The academics tell us that children are abused in a number of ways and it may appear to them to be a ‘loving’ relationship. Four categories are widely recognised today: physical abuse, emotional abuse, sexual abuse and neglect.[2] It is only now that I can see that the abuse I experienced was mainly in the first three categories. But the trauma a child, or an adult, experiences in any one of these categories is significant and deep. In the last twenty-five years medical science has started to catch up, although currently only limited training is given to doctors. Specialists like Judith Herman have documented their research lifting the lid and allowing us to appreciate what has happened.

‘The traumatised person ... frequently alternates between isolation and anxiously clinging to others ... Traumatised people suffer damage to the basic structures of the self. They lose their trust in themselves, in other people, and in God. Their self-esteem is assaulted by experiences of humiliation, guilt, and helplessness. Their capacity for intimacy is compromised by intense and contradictory feelings of need and fear.’[3]

Men and women who manage to speak about their experience will often refer to the frustration of isolation. They will say, ‘If I had been in an accident, people would see the damage. Because this is all on the inside it is unseen, unknown and not understood.’

The quotes from Dr.Judith Herman above and at the start of this chapter, describe some of damage from this evil crime. No wonder Jesus gave a deadly warning to anyone who stops children from getting close to Him.

‘If anyone causes one of these little ones—those who believe in me—to stumble, it would be better for them to have a large millstone hung around their neck and to be drowned in the depths of the sea.’ (Matthew 18:6)

Chapter 2

Picture a mother taking her small girl Christmas shopping. They are in a large department store and mummy has just helped her daughter to buy a present for her friend. While queuing at the tills, the little girl is distracted and lured away by a man. He snatches the present so violently from her grasp that her wrist is dislocated and tendons are torn. Christmases would never be the same again.

Let us be clear about this. What the sexual predator steals is part of the life of their victim. It is not a sexual experience alone that has been stolen. It is that gift which is part of the soul or the personality which has been dislocated and torn away too. The abuser believes that he (or she) is taking what is natural because to them it is understood to be a 'loving relationship'. In many cases, they have conned their victim into believing the same. Could the sexual predator's dark deception of a 'loving relationship', this fundamental lie, be shattered by knowing they are about to seriously injure a person's personality and cause a deformity that, without constructive intervention, may last the rest of their lives?

Thousands of adults have experienced far greater traumas than mine, and thousands of children live in a far darker nightmare. What confused me was that those who wielded such painful experiences on me were involved in cathedral life, in the choir or in the clergy. Also, the sexual activity was in the context of friendship. The bargaining chip was extra attention; a highly valued commodity. Through this pseudo-love I was won into a sexual experience that I perceived as inevitable and perhaps normal. I have wonderful parents and they were obviously unaware of what was happening at boarding school.

Leaving boarding school at the age of thirteen, I began a different adventure at the local mixed secondary school. The contrast was startling. I survived lessons that were often beyond the teacher's control and avoided the teenage trainee gangsters by using a number of ploys. Now of course there were girls! Although I fancied a number of girls, I couldn't approach them because I was shy. In my eyes, I simply didn't measure up to the witty, sporty, academic, talented, attractive, healthy-looking teens around me. So, I did not have a girlfriend until I was seventeen. When I eventually woke up to a world where I was acceptable to the opposite sex, pleasure became my choice drug. Sexual promiscuity, alcohol and drug abuse, with a relentless perfectionism, dominated my late teens and early twenties.

Life appeared to be sweet but it was just a sugar coating. Under the coating, I was feeding a well-hidden and vile smelling monster. There followed severe mood swings, feelings of abandonment, occasional bursts of destructive anger, and episodes of deep depression with thoughts of suicide. I cruelly broke off one relationship when I went to college. Two years later, my fiancée broke off our engagement because I had been unfaithful. There were many other girlfriends and the physical comfort in having one girlfriend after another kept the monster tranquillised.

Underneath the surface of my creative, polished exterior was a desperate, emotional, demanding, lonely, comfort-craving addict. Excessive drinking and physical pleasure pacified the emotional pain and the anger of the inner monster. These are quite typical symptoms that lie behind a variety of serious addictions.[4]

Life after abuse is not without its high spots, but there are now a new set of emotions that are at best difficult or at worst impossible to tame. These may be immediate, or may not surface for some time. Distancing or disassociation can be spotted in children by those who are aware of this. The dislocated or torn personality can be clearly seen in particular patterns of behaviour.[5]

Children have a multitude of great capacities but they are neither tough nor resilient. What they are good at is wearing disguises. Like chameleons, they cover their problems in the hope of blending in with the crowd and being accepted. This gives an appearance of being adaptable, resilient and of being alright. Most children want to please the adults around them and not kick up a fuss. Other children express themselves with unsociable behaviour. These are obviously not chameleons but uncontrollable terriers. Both chameleons and terriers have underlying issues that can stay unaddressed. Tragically, research is showing that trauma affects emotional maturity, and the emotional stage of development at the time of abuse can be where the survivor stays in their emotions.[6]

The symptoms following abuse (which we return to in chapter 6) are like a class of unruly teenagers being managed by a survivor with the undeveloped emotions of a child. With no knowledge of how to do this, the survivor resorts to some sophisticated and dangerous coping mechanisms; anything to distract from or deaden the pain. Being a workaholic or perfectionist, alcoholic, drug addict, self-harmer, or helping others, fighting for a cause, hiding in a community are all common coping mechanisms. But until the underlying symptoms have been addressed, these coping mechanisms simply keep a lid on the trauma. The worms under the lid squirm away, alive as ever.

We must not lose sight of this: a survivor is a remarkable individual managing all the complexities and fallout of childhood abuse. Many have developed their own strategies to manage themselves, to raise families, to hold down jobs, to be useful in their communities, and often have an enlarged capacity to care for others empathetically. We should recognise their creativity, intelligence and determination. They truly are amazing people. Whether a survivor appears to hold everything together or their world is constantly falling apart, they share something in common. There is a distortion of the real person.

Jesus always deeply respected the person with unfathomable compassion while reaching with truth the 'demon issues' in their life. I am certain that he would embrace the little girl in the shop closely with acceptance, give her present back to her and bring healing to every displaced bone and every torn tendon. We do not have his capacity (nor obviously his divinity), but hope for the hopeless is born as we learn to look at the downtrodden and abused in the way he does. That hope then grows strong and healthy as we live and work the way he did.

To come to terms with past issues of child abuse takes great courage and great humility, both of which I have lacked. Courage and humility are like two fuel tanks needed for the long haul of recovery and must never run on empty. Only the Lord can keep refuelling us with the fuel of his grace and love. He alone helps us to be courageous when people find it hard to understand and may stigmatise us. He alone helps us to humble ourselves when we are vulnerable to pride in what we think we have achieved. Courage and humility allow us to cling to the teachings of Jesus.[7] As we cling, we find it possible to replace our inadequate coping mechanisms with his truth and so be set free.

A new day is dawning

> 'See, I am doing a new thing! Now it springs up; do you not perceive it? I am making a way in the desert and streams in the waste land.'
>
> Isaiah 43:19.

At the age of eighteen, I was given a card after a Christian rock concert inviting me to a young people's organisation called 'The Jesus Liberation Front'. I was revising for my A Level exams and became depressed. I opened my desk drawer and contemplated cutting my wrists with a Stanley knife. I didn't know at the time that suicidal thoughts can be typical of those who have been abused. But there, next to the knife, was the invitation card. I decided to go to their base and said to the Lord, 'If you are really there, prove yourself to me.' The impact of God's love when I met these Christians was almost overwhelming.

Many things changed that day but some of the underlying issues didn't. At this stage, I have to tell you that chunks of my behaviour continued long after being 'born from above' when I was eighteen. God lovingly broke through my resistance to him and overcame all the concerns I had about the Bible.

One of many favourite texts for me is Galatians 2:20:

> 'I have been crucified with Christ. It is no longer I who live, but Christ who lives in me. And the life I now live in the flesh I live by faith in the Son of God, who loved me and gave Himself for me.'

I can therefore say that these issues and those events are dead in Christ. I know that I no longer have the unbearable burden of trying to make myself acceptable to God. I know that the old Robert and everything he has done or had done to him is dead. Instead I now trust Christ to guide and to strengthen me for everything I do. At the cross, my Lord Jesus took the punishment for my sin in his own body. I know that it is gone and can praise God that I am free.

However, it would seem that I have not been quite as free as I should be. I have found this frustrating and somewhat embarrassing. It took Jesus various stages to give sight to a blind man who at first saw trees.[1] Why should it not take time to go to the depths of my issues? I have had to learn that God is beyond our time frames and way above our expectations.

Sue knew that I had been abused while at boarding school. I mentioned it in passing before we got married. But neither of us recognised the impact on our relationship until we read Judith Herman's book. We didn't connect my bizarre behaviour to the childhood trauma.

To have the child abuse out in the open is comforting but to understand how it had affected Sue was devastating. We decided to go for counselling. Being open brought us a brand new dawn but it also brought fresh light to see the monster that I felt I was. In an overwhelming sense of disgust and disgrace I was struggling to know what to do to put this right. What could I do to correct this and then make up for the lost years? What a mess. I was facing some major adjustments and at the same time trying to support Sue who was understandably depressed. This was one of the lowest points for both of us.

Over the years Sue and I have made a number of attempts to resolve underlying problems: prayer counselling, biblical counselling and conferences. Each of these have been helpful but not one of them touched the depth of the underlying problem. I have been privileged both to counsel others with complex problems and be alongside some of Christendom's well-known leaders. Through self-discipline, I have held myself in check often with innovative techniques derived from scriptural principles. That self-discipline, learnt so well through boarding school, and the techniques derived from scriptural principles, enabled me to keep it all 'under wraps'.

Some raised the issue of demonic possession. As a young Christian, and later as a student minister, we confronted demonic activity. We did not go looking for demons. They surfaced from people without invitation. I think that anyone can have a demon but this is far from the norm. Abused children can mistakenly be thought to have a demon. Their bizarre behaviour arises from their feeling of being outside themselves (dissociation), and numbing the emotions is a form of protection and is often accompanied by memory loss and mental illness. They are helped when treated as such and not as demonic. It would obviously be tragic to try and cast out a dissociative state!

In my morning devotion, I read about King David and how, his son, Absalom's treachery against him had concluded. The exact opposite of what he wanted had happened. He asked the troops to be gentle with Absalom yet he was speared to death while hanging in a tree.[2] David is now grieving deeply, but he has to put this aside to rally and comfort the troops who were dejected and humiliated.[3] Joab, the king's number one commander, knew the mood of the troops and told David that while he was ripped apart with grief, the troops felt devastated, unwanted and unappreciated. David rallied. Once more he won their hearts and they wanted him to rule over them. In this extreme experience, the Lord helped David to take the right steps to recover the situation from the brink of disaster. He had to suspend his own grief to do the right thing. I also knew I was to learn the same lesson as David and do the same as him.

I do not usually experience such vivid dreams, but during that night of wrestling with sleeplessness referred to in chapter 1, I eventually slept, and in my dream, I heard these words of Jesus clearly and strongly: 'Come to Me, all you who are weary and burdened and I will give you rest.'[4] David had also found the Lord was right there in his extreme experience. With Jesus, there is always hope even when we are experiencing pain which is tearing us apart. I had to tell myself: 'The Lord, and not a person, is taking us through this. He is the great physician of our soul and can restore us from shame, from grief and humiliation. He will also help us to put aside our personal grief to rally and comfort others'. A new day was dawning. I was convinced that the Lord was going to do a new thing. The journey of restoration was about to begin.

Section 2
Restored—The journey of restoration

'Don't judge yourself by what others did to you.'
C. Kennedy

The tough journey—getting to the root of the issues

'Though the soul's wounds heal; the scars remain. God sees them not as blemishes but as honours.'

Julian of Norwich, *Revelations of Divine Love*

Mr. Springit, who taught me maths, insisted that everyone in his class had to understand a concept before he would move on to the next one. When I taught teenagers, I learned they needed to taste success to go to the next level. This approach became the seed that grew into what I later called the 'crest of a wave' philosophy. Small successes put them onto the crest of a wave. Then they could tackle future challenges from a place of success and not from a trough of failure.

Small but significant steps forward that give some success, are at the core of the messy journey of restoration. The Lord patiently shows us how to succeed so that we have a new confidence in Him. As we cling to Him, He shows us truths that we understand in our lives. These new understandings put us onto the crest of a wave. Then we are more able to let Him help us to tackle bigger challenges. We crash into troughs and fall, but that taste of success helps us to cling to Jesus all over again. Bit by bit we are taking steps to being set free.[1]

The toughest times are when a wave of emotions sweep over us like a tsunami: 'Tamar put ashes on her head and tore the ornamented robe she was wearing. She put her hand on her head and went away, weeping aloud as she went.'[2] Tamar had just been raped by her brother. She mourned openly as if she was grieving the death of someone she loved. Those who have been abused might subdue their feelings, imprisoning them in a deep dark dungeon so that they cannot see the light of day. Those who haven't imprisoned their feelings might struggle at times to know what to do with them. These feelings can be so devastating, intense, unreasonable and destructive that they have been described as a tsunami.

We might tell ourselves that we should not have feelings like this. But why? Aren't these same feelings described in the Bible? King David certainly had strong feelings even to the point of saying, 'my heart fails me.'[3] It is not having feelings that is the issue, but what is done with them. Not all feelings are right. Some are clearly wrong, and we will consider this later. The term some writers use is a 'fragile process'. This is when something makes a person feel vulnerable or fragile and overwhelmed. There is an inability to process the feelings in the past so as to live in the present. Apparently, this can be common for those who went to boarding school, as well as for those who have been abused. They are in effect being made to grow up too soon which makes the child more vulnerable and open to a perpetrator wanting to exploit them. I never blamed my parents, and always wanted to spare them from knowing what had happened. They are respectable members of the community and were, and are, good parents.

There is also a sense of desertion. Abandonment is a cruel, irrational and destructive feeling. The cause is understandable. But it is not straightforward to see through the mess of emotions. Every time it erupts, abandonment needs replacing with a revelation of God's love. Easy to say, but not easy to do. The powerful horror of abandonment can be overcome with the greater power of divine love: 'When my father and my mother forsake me, then the LORD will take me up.'[4]

What can I do? My own desire was to repair all this. 'No, not repair', I was told by one counsellor and was given this quote from Julian of Norwich's *Revelations of Divine Love*:

> 'Though the soul's wounds heal; the scars remain. God sees them not as blemishes but as honours.'

I needed to accept that I would live with scar tissue until the day I die. This was deeply disturbing, until I saw that Jesus still has his scars. These constantly remind us of the price of his 'crest of the wave' triumph. He has come through the worst abuse imaginable so that he can restore us to a relationship with His Father. There is, of course, a big difference between my repair job and the restorative work of Jesus.

When a tsunami of emotions sweeps over me this is what I tell myself.

- Don't expect anyone else to do anything. How can someone who has never been in this tsunami know what to do? This is my tsunami. I must take charge of my response to it and I badly need the Lord to help me.

- Step aside and ask, 'What's happening?' This is a tough challenge. But write things down because it really helps. So, journal what is happening. Try to be calm in speaking to others and do not accuse them. By controlled communication you might be able to explain what you are feeling and ask for prayer. If there is no apparent reason for this tsunami, then accept that and think of good times, or something else to distract your thinking.
- Do something constructive; something you would like to do. Channel these emotions into something that is good; build a model or do some cooking, go for a walk or a run, sing along with some praise songs, go to an event that will absorb you, or watch a helpful film. Anything that takes your mind into something different. For some it is having a significant time alone with the Lord. Have something ready for these times. It could be something that you used to enjoy as a child or wished you had done as a child.

I soon became aware that overwhelming feelings or no feelings at all are part of the journey. Both have their dangers. Wounds do heal and we will see that God intends to bind up and heal the broken heart. The scars however, remain and can be an irritation.

Our hope for the future is set on what God tells us; when he gives us his word, it cannot be broken. Words like: 'God restores the years that the locusts have eaten.'[5] Jesus tells us that he is in our journey of restoration: 'If you hold (or cling) to my teaching, you are really my disciples. Then you will know the truth, and the truth will set you free … if the Son sets you free you will be free indeed.'[6]

If I cling to Jesus and His teachings, as a true disciple I will then appreciate fully His teachings and they will set me free. I will be radically and truly free because it will be Jesus who does it. So, if I am not free from tsunamis right now it could be that a particular truth has not yet lit up my mind. The penny has not yet dropped! But if I am willing, Jesus has said that the penny will drop. He will make sure of it.

Over the next few chapters, we open up a journey which gradually restores our life from being a victim to being a survivor. Then, further on, to being a 'thriver' whose wounds are healed but whose scars remain.

Chapter 5

Crucial truths that set us free

'Truth, like gold, is to be obtained not by its growth, but by washing away from it all that is not gold.'

Leo Tolstoy

If you are a survivor then I would like to tell you that you are an amazing person—true gold. Your sensitivity, insights, your abilities, and your durable character are just a few of the extraordinary things about you. It has taken many years for this to 'sink in' to my thinking so that I am only just genuinely accepting it. But there are unique abilities that survivors have developed since they were abused. You may not agree with this so please read on.

From an early age, I wanted to be an artist. I love making things; from model kits to restoring an old stone cottage in France. I spent quite a few happy years teaching teenagers art, among other things. One girl had made a top-grade clay sculpture of a mother and child, which exploded in the kiln. I spent hours gluing it back together again and filling the cracks before she saw it. You couldn't tell it had been blown into dozens of pieces because we used acrylic paint to make it look like bronze. The cracks could not be seen. So, I had a nagging question: 'Why has the Lord allowed this major flaw in my life with the potential of wrecking everything?'

The Lord put the blue print together and then sculpted my life. This includes my characteristics, personality, skills and abilities. These components are me. He is the designer and artist. But what about the flaws, and specifically this flaw in my emotions? I had just preached Romans 8:28 so the answer was right there: 'And we know that in all things God works for the good of those who love him, who have been called according to his purpose.' Had I been called according to His purpose; and did I love Him? Well, yes, of course. There is no question about it. Was He also at work in my life?

Since a very early age I have been aware that God is at work in my life. So, God is in it all. But it is more than this, I had to challenge myself again: 'Do you know, really know, so that you *know*?' 'Yes', I had to answer. Even in times of doubt I have the nagging certainty that God is at the centre of it all. But then there is the crunch: that little word 'ALL'. Do I know that God is working ALL things together for my good? I have always wanted to say for *his* good and glory but Paul doesn't actually say that in Romans 8:28.

Do I accept that God is orchestrating every aspect of my life and everything going on inside me to bring about my good right now and then for eternity? Can my Lord Jesus take all the misery of abandonment down the years and orchestrate it for my good? That is a tough one. The thing I had to accept was that He already has. And because He is the same and never changes, He always will. In fact, God works on His people like a potter shaping a lifeless lump of clay.[1] The Israelites saw the potter at work every day in their villages. This is the way it is. God shapes our lives—not to our timing nor to our outcomes, but all to his.

Do you find it difficult to believe what I have just said? So often I catch myself living and speaking against this truth. How can I (or we if you are joining me on this) live more fully in the stunning beauty of our Master-crafted lives? How can we get a better hold on what heaven's perspective is? I really don't want to wait till I get to heaven to hear words like: 'Wasn't I telling you this all along?' Can I accept God's work washing away all that is not gold to expose his eternal gold?

What I needed to accept from the Master-Creator was this:

Firstly, I am an awesome creation because God is an awesome Creator.

King David wrote, 'I praise you because I am fearfully and wonderfully made ...'[2] and this speaks loudly down the centuries to our hearts today. God Himself sculpted me in the studio of my mother's womb. The results were awesome and wonder-filled! He was fully aware of what he saw, and always will be as he sees things all the time even in the depths of our darkest night. David does something that is so important; he praises the Lord for the good job that he has done and how amazing He is.[3]

It is tough for survivors to accept that they are awesome. Those who have not been abused may also find this hard to accept. Some fuse has blown in the electrical circuitry of our basic love and trust which needs replacing. God is able to do this work instantaneously and, if he chooses, completely. I do not doubt this for a second. But for many of us it is a slow, gradual, journey of restoration and not a complete recovery. All I can say at this stage is that I accelerated that journey by making a habit of praising God for the wonderful job he did in creating me. It starts with the Lord saying something like this: 'I am not asking you to love yourself, nor accept that others could love you. What I am asking you to do is to absorb into your heart what I say about you.'

Secondly, I have been given a life which God has prepared and permitted in every part.

This is not easy for me to say, but accept it I must. To do this, I need God's help. If you're joining me on this journey, we need to cry out to God for his grace. Right now, let us pray, 'Lord, please give me your grace to see this, so that the penny will drop!' King David also wrote: 'All the days ordained for me were written in your book before one of them came to be.'[4] There is that difficult word 'All' again. I clench my teeth at this but I must believe that what was true for David is true for me. ALL my days (however many that is), have been ordained by God and even written about in his book before even one of them came to be. There is a chapter in God's book in heaven about my life.[5] God is good and a great Creator. He has designed us and sculpted us in every part and has brought us to himself to make us his own possession.

Thirdly, I am chosen by God, made holy by Him and dearly loved by Him.

A couple of days after working on this we had a text from our eldest daughter. She wanted us to read Colossians 3:12. 'You are chosen by God; you are made holy by God; and you are dearly loved by God ...' (see also Colossians 1:22). In this verse, there are three things that I should not lose sight of on my journey. I could then tell myself this each day and when certain emotions started to creep back. How easy it was to skim over the depth of these truths. Eternal truths which are like that 'crest of a wave' impetus (in Chapter 4) that God wants us to have so that we can do the things that follow on after this verse. What are those eternal truths?

God decided who His children should be.

We did not choose Him or decide to follow Him. At the core of our relationship with our heavenly Father and our new spiritual life is this profound fact. God, out of His own will, decided that we would belong to him as his adopted child. He made his mind up and set his love on us before the world was ever formed.[6] There was nothing we did to influence him, but it has always been everything he does that influences us.

God took the initiative to make me holy.

It is no coincidence that Moses, and later Joshua, were commanded by God to take off their sandals to stand on holy ground.7 Through the sacrifice they offered he would wipe away all the sin ever committed against him. Not just because of their rebellion against him but because of their natural state that is born diseased with sin. The crucifixion of God the Son, foreshadowed in the sacrifices offered by Moses and Joshua, was the only way God the Father could reconcile his chosen people to Himself. This is how he could bring people like us into his all-Holy presence. By this truly awesome and bloody execution, God demonstrates his unfathomable love and his perfect justice for all eternity. He makes his adopted children perfectly holy in his sight 'Without spot or blemish'.8

God loves me more dearly than I will ever be able to comprehend in this life.

God's love is much more than passion and beautiful feelings. His love is the determination of his will to do what is ultimately the best for others. We can find glimpses of love like this in the heroic lives and actions of selfless individuals. But these, no matter how great, will only be gentle shadows of the all-powerful magnificence of God's love.

I wrote those verses from Psalm 139 and Colossians 3 on a pocket size piece of card and turned to it a few times a day. It was a struggle at times, but having lived with it for week and then a month, the penny dropped. The Lord brings change and reveals his truth. By keeping what God says in front of us and not what others say (or our thoughts tell us or the enemy brings), our minds are renewed and that leads us into transformation. God washes away the filth to bring through his deposit of gold. He, as the master craftsman, puts the pieces of his works of art back together.

Chapter 6

The Reality Check—what is it really like?

'A man is not known by his effervescence but by the amount of real suffering he can stand.'

C.T.Studd, missionary to central Africa

'The Lord is a refuge for the oppressed, a stronghold in times of trouble. Those who know your name will trust in you, for you O Lord, have never forsaken those who seek you' (King David, Psalm 9:9–10).

I heard a musician on the radio say, 'All musicians fail. All you can do is fail better!' Whatever our taste in music we bathe something deep in our emotions with their art. We are accustomed to a continual stream of auditory perfection. When mistakes are made publicly, they stand out like an explosion on the landscape of our hearing. But behind the scenes there are blunders, miss-timings, struggles to master the difficult parts and frustrations when things go wrong. In the recording studio, errors can be edited so we never know the blunders. It's just like the cleanup job that is done on photographs with an airbrush. Imperfections are skilfully removed.

This is what we do with our lives. I was reminded about this when my daughter, in her new job, faced her first call-out to a child abuse case. It was a shock and an emotional time as she came to terms with the ugliness of something that is usually hidden in our society. There is something so vile, so ugly, so disturbing that even though we may know that it happens and always has, we airbrush it out of our lives. It's time to face an unedited recording or a non-airbrushed picture. The victim of abuse controlled by a selfish perpetrator should no longer be put away from our sight like the insane in the Victorian asylums.

Let me paint the truer picture for you. You will realise I'm sure, that it is not the picture that every survivor would present if they were listened to.

But there will be some common characteristics. What is it really like for a survivor without the airbrushing?

It is a reoccurring deep-seated fear of being controlled again and a fight never to allow that to happen. When it is not fear of being controlled, it is an anxiety of being abandoned. When it is not the anxiety of being abandoned it is the hopelessness of not seeing any way out. When it is not the hopelessness it can be the anger at the injustice of it all: 'How could a trusted adult misuse me?' When it is not the anger, it is the feeling of being the odd one out, different from other 'normal' people. Fear, anxiety, hopelessness, depression, self-loathing and more. These emotions throw themselves up unexpectedly like plastic rubbish on the shore of daily life for you to collect up and deal with so that the beach is kept clear. At times, it is overwhelming.

It is a longing to be with people and talk incessantly to forget, but then to withdraw and be alone because you cannot face people. You want to be close to the people you love but are tripped up by the feelings of intense need or the fear of failure.

It is a struggle with the distrust of people and often those who are an authority figure or who are loved ones: 'I know I should trust this person but what if they let me down?' 'Will I be able to handle the reoccurrence of destructive emotions?'

Then there are the sleepless nights, the gaps in memory, the abject loneliness that is often self-created because you are a demanding person to be with, the interruption of intimacy with your spouse, upset stomachs, through to despair and yes, suicidal thoughts: 'Wouldn't it be best for everyone if I just end it?'

There are other ways to explain it that some survivors would use:

It is like living with an enemy who perpetually abuses these emotions and who needs to be fought off otherwise he takes the ground of your security, well-being and happiness.

It is like being down in the dumps on the inside but positive on the outside. A regular and at times a constant depression that seems unreasonable because sometimes there is no reason to be depressed.

It is an uphill struggle, similar to mourning the death of a loved one. Tears can be just under the surface. Conversely, such a tight grip can be holding emotions that they die. The emotional pain can leave you physically weak and exhausted. The emotional deadness leaves you detached and empty against degrees of emotions (from mild up to a tsunami intensity) and the need to freeze them out with denial or pacify them with addictions.

This is an ugly picture, isn't it? But this is something of the never-usually-spoken-of that is behind the scenes in some people's life.

Chart 1 puts in diagram form the heinous mess of fallout from sexual abuse.

This emotional tsunami shows the ugly swings and roundabouts that can be experienced. The remarkable thing is that many survivors manage all of this with a creative tenacity of a war hero. People we know can also be PTSD sufferers. Where everything is now out of balance, modern medicine can get back some equilibrium with chemicals, and this is sometimes necessary. As a layman, I suspect that these can quiet the emotions but not touch the problem.

You may be someone who has not experienced any of this, but you want to understand and offer help to those who have. If that is the case I suggest you pause and just thank God that you have not been abused. Then please, do your best get a realistic picture of those who have.

If you have experienced childhood (or adult) abuse and you are reading this and identifying: 'This has happened to me' or 'This is describing something of what my real inner life is like.' Remember, 'All musicians fail. All you can do is fail better!'

So, we need to try to be realistic in our views and in our expectations. How can we do this?

I am training myself to be realistic in this way. It is God who brings change and we need to co-operate with Him in, what we perceive as, our failures. There is no shame in making mistakes when your heart is set on moving forward. For some of us there is a certain hope not necessarily a complete cure. We will one day be like Christ when we see him face to face. In the meantime, we live as close to him as is humanly possible and see some changes, some progress and some failures. There is restoration not full recovery.

No one should be given more cruelty with empty promises. God does miracles, and you may be someone who receives a miracle from God to bring complete transformation, instantly. Some people have wonderful and impressive stories of what God has done. This is God's decision and

CHART 1 The Heinous Mess of Child/Sexual Abuse: An Emotional Tsunami

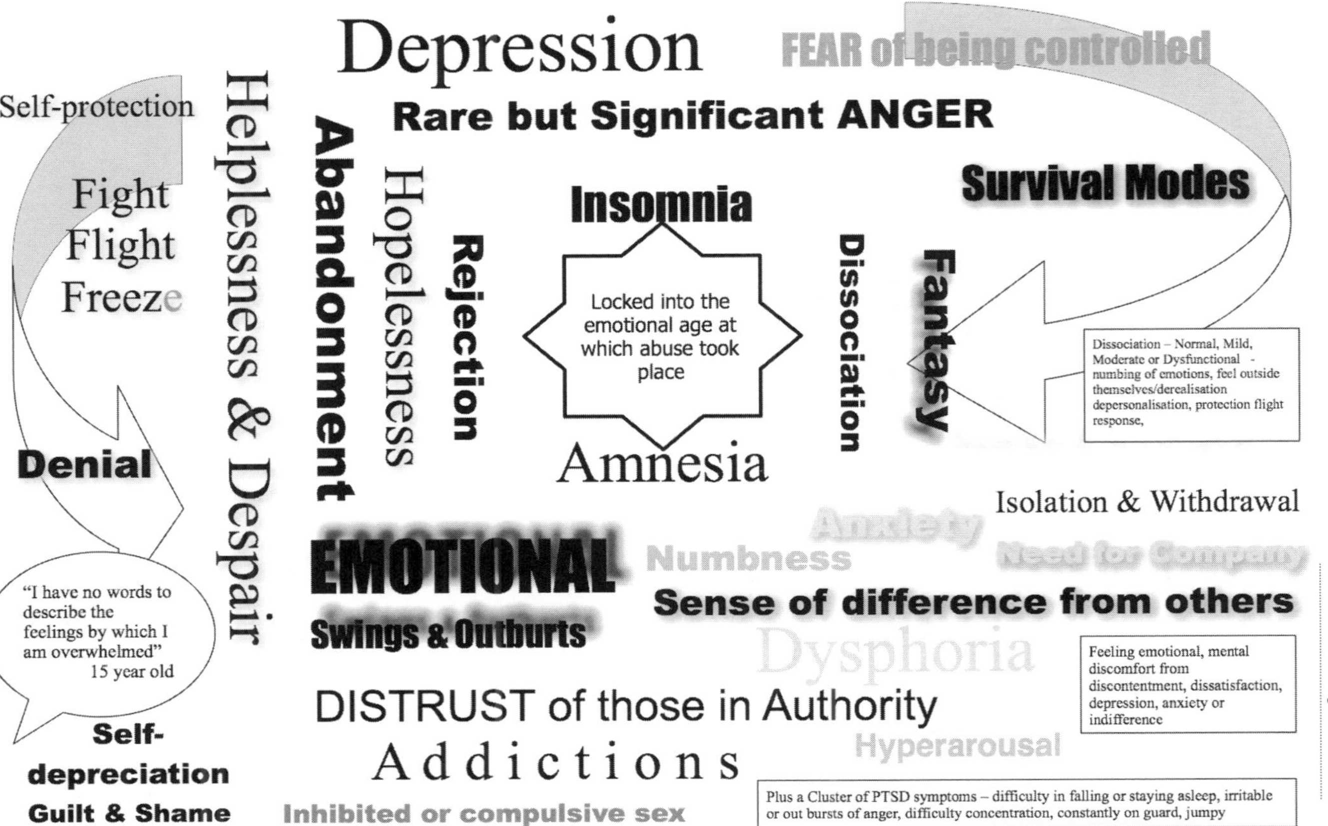
Depression
FEAR of being controlled
Rare but Significant ANGER
Self-protection
Fight
Flight
Freeze
Helplessness & Despair
Abandonment
Hopelessness
Rejection
Insomnia
Locked into the emotional age at which abuse took place
Amnesia
Dissociation
Fantasy
Survival Modes
Dissociation – Normal, Mild, Moderate or Dysfunctional - numbing of emotions, feel outside themselves/derealisation depersonalisation, protection flight response,
Denial
"I have no words to describe the feelings by which I am overwhelmed" 15 year old
Self-depreciation
Guilt & Shame
EMOTIONAL
Swings & Outburts
Isolation & Withdrawal
Anxiety
Numbness
Need for Company
Sense of difference from others
Dysphoria
Feeling emotional, mental discomfort from discontentment, dissatisfaction, depression, anxiety or indifference
DISTRUST of those in Authority
Hyperarousal
Addictions
Inhibited or compulsive sex
Plus a Cluster of PTSD symptoms – difficulty in falling or staying asleep, irritable or out bursts of anger, difficulty concentration, constantly on guard, jumpy

not yours or mine. Jesus miraculously healed a few, but not everyone. The reality of His ministry is that there was a great deal that He did not do, and needs he did not meet. What the New Testament records is changed lives: 'And that is what some of you were.'[1] The Christians at Corinth, who Paul was writing to here, knew that God had made this major change in their lives. But they would need to co-operate with God to have ongoing changes so that they could move forward. In this way, we will fail a lot better by being realistic about the 'ups and downs' of change.

One thing I was determined about, was that my children would not be affected by my experiences. The abuse would stop with me. There is a myth that those who have been victims of abuse will go on to be perpetrators themselves. The research I have found shows that it is actually a small percentage of victims who become perpetrators.[2]

Child abuse leaves the victim with deep scarring, distorted thinking and a zoo full of wild emotions. We have hope. There is hope for gradual transforming changes. These are often found in obvious and unexpected places.

Chapter 7

You are not alone—our hero's cry too

'While it is good to walk among the living, it is good also to live with the wise, great, and good dead … It makes us always know that God made other men before he made us … It provides us with perpetual humility and inspiration.'

Brooks, quoted by Warren Wiersbe[1]

What a discovery! We can benefit by getting close to the struggles of our Bible heroes (instead of worshipping them at a distance). Inner struggles are especially difficult for those of us who think that because we are Christians we should be living a life of victory and joy all the time. However, Paul, Peter, Elijah, Moses, Joshua, Jonah, Isaiah, Jeremiah and, on one or two occasions, Jesus Himself, all had inner struggles. Despair, severe depression, anxiety, tears, suicidal thoughts are some of their experiences.

One of my favourites is King David. In the lyrics he wrote for his songs (or Psalms), his experience of deep emotion is plain to see. What he also learnt to do really well—most of the time—was to take his experience to the Lord and place his dependence on Him. That doesn't necessarily make us feel better. The jingle tune on the ice cream van is the same every time. We can hear this same response from well-meaning friends: 'Trust the Lord. You've got to trust the Lord.' It's the right thing to say but just recognising the tune doesn't always deliver the ice cream!

David tells things as they really are, but he had also learnt his 'trust lesson' well. Don't let this put you off. David had been trusting the Lord and doing some amazing things since he was a child. As God's children, our inner compass-point always goes back to North—to God. David's seems to return quicker because he had been doing it most of his life.

This is a sample chart from Appendix 1 of David's real experience. The picture without airbrushing is on the left. I've given a title to his emotions, so that we can see them clearly. He speaks openly about his inner struggles and what he does with them. Here are three examples of the complaints, concerns and open emotions he verbalises to God. I revisit the full chart of David's experiences and responses regularly and find that it gives hope and direction.

THE REAL KING DAVID: THE FOLLOWING VERSES ARE ALL FROM THE PSALMS.	
DAVID'S EXPERIENCE	DAVID'S RESPONSE
Deeply troubled and Desperate » 'My soul is in **anguish**. How long, O Lord, how long?' » 'I am **worn out** from groaning, all night long I flood my bed with weeping and drench my couch with tears' (6:3,6)	» 'My shield is God Most High' » 'I will give thanks to the Lord because of his righteousness and will sing praise to the name of the Lord Most High.' (7:10,17) » 'The Lord is a refuge for the oppressed, a stronghold in times of trouble.' (9:9)
Deserted and vulnerable to evil men » 'Help, Lord, for no one is faithful any more; those who are loyal have vanished from the human race.' » '... the wicked who freely strut about when **what is vile is honoured** by the human race' (12:1,8)	» 'Because the poor are plundered and the needy groan, I will now arise,' says the Lord. 'I will protect them from those who malign them.' » 'You, Lord, will keep the needy safe and will protect us for ever from the wicked,' (12:5,7)
	» 'Keep me safe, my God for in you I take refuge.''**I keep my eyes always on the Lord. With him at my right hand, I shall not be shaken.** Therefore my heart is glad and my tongue rejoices; my body also will rest secure ..' (16:1,8,9, whole Psalm)

What are some of the lessons we can learn from the way David handled his emotions?

Desperate lows can be turned into determined highs.

David has his low spots where he openly tells God, and us, that he is depressed, broken, helpless, isolated and alone, distressed, overcome with fear or anxiety, exhausted, in emotional pain, vulnerable, desperate, physically ill and on the point of death. But he also seems to counter these times with a great determination to be absorbed with the Lord. Not easy, I know.

Distrusting our emotions can lead to a deeper dependence on the Lord.

This is a hard one, but it would seem that David did this. He openly acknowledges his experience but then prays bluntly and praises exuberantly. He asks God, even tells him, to deal with people who are opposing him. Then he praises God so enthusiastically that he is more conscious of God than of his troubles. Sounds great, doesn't it? Let's be realistic and remember that David has a lifetime of training under his belt because he has been doing this from childhood. We need to find ways of getting this approach of praising God into our lives. How can this be done?

In wanting to be like David, I have learnt to turn round on my challenges and fight them with prayer and praise. Psalm 149:6–9 describes this. David often did this by bookending his challenges with praise that declared what God is like. We find him doing this in Psalm 18 when he had slipped away from King Saul, who had pursued him into the desert, where David was hiding. Two verses near the beginning and at the end of the psalm (3 and 46) stand out as his bookends.

There are major lessons I need to learn from David's triumphs and his blunders. At the very point of those low spots, David turns himself around with a great determination to be absorbed with the Lord. When will I learn that the Lord is more than ready to absorb me?

Chapter 8

The Doctor of our broken heart

'Grace conquers us first, and we, by it conquer all else; whether corruptions within us, or temptations from outside us.'

Richard Sibbes, the Puritan in *The Bruised Reed*

Where can I find comfort in my brokenness? I need an answer to that question. Our comfort blankets are an attractive solution. But they are just a quick fix that compounds the problem and makes a greater mess.

What did Jesus do when faced with a crowd who were beaten down by their religious experience? He saw their exhaustion and how they were weighed down by their burdens, and gave them an offer that they really shouldn't be able to refuse. Again and again these words invite me with the same compassion and power with which Jesus spoke to them on that day: '*Come to me, all* you who are weary and burdened, and *I will* give you *rest*'.[1]

This is a deep and profound spiritual rest from all our struggles to be right with God. It is a rest in the sufficient and complete work that Christ achieved on the cross to wipe away our sin so that we can be right with God. Right on His terms and by his sacrifice alone. This also must include rest for us from all that sin has done to us. I mean, the sin that has been cruelly forced on us by a perpetrator. Sin which is not ours, but theirs. Sin that we have wrongly carried and has been an unbearable burden to us throughout the years. Jesus says, 'I *will* give you rest.'

How can we know that this is what Jesus does? Well, this is what he became human to do. When the Lord Jesus came to earth, from His perfect glory in heaven, He made His mission statement abundantly clear. You will find it in Isaiah 61:1–3. He was anointed by the Father to:

- proclaim his good news to those who were poor and wretched,

- to wrap round securely the broken hearted,
- to announce freedom for those captured by different issues and release those shut away blinded in a variety of dark prisons,
- and to make it clear that this is *now*.

I know I qualify for this. Do you? Do you feel poor and wretched in yourself, brokenhearted, captured by your past experiences as if you have been imprisoned? Jesus brings a deep comfort to everyone who is mourning or grieving among his people. He then replaces their grief with praise. They have their heads anointed with the oil of rejoicing to re-place their mourning, and put on clothes of praise to God instead of their rags of despair. God will do such a significant and thorough work in them that they will then be seen as strong 'Oaks of righteousness', displaying his own splendour in them.

Wow—all of this!

Can you believe this is what Jesus does? This is why Jesus could say, 'Come to *me*' and promise a rest only He could give. Only Jesus could make this promise. Only he can bind up the broken hearted like this.

There is no doubt in my mind that survivors need something more than a glib, 'Trust in Jesus.' We need to know what it is to receive His gift into the very centre of our unexplainable pain. We need nothing less than His power and anointing which he only can apply because he is the doctor of our soul; a spiritual work in us by the Holy Spirit. I pray the following words often. Would you like to read these words as your prayer?

> 'Lord Jesus, anointed One, let me know Your good news, bind up my broken heart, speak freedom to my captured heart and comfort my grieving heart. Put on me a crown of beauty, the oil of gladness, and wedding clothes of praise instead of the ashes of grieving. Name me as one of Your oaks of righteousness to display Your splendour through my new life. Amen.'

What Julian of Norwich said troubles me. Is she right when she said, 'Though the wounds heal, the scars remain. God sees them not as blemishes but as honours'?

One question that had bothered me is why has it taken forty-five years to expose this root cause of many of my problems? Scar tissue can indeed restrict movement. But when we see the Lord healing people, He did a thorough job. I skip-read Matthew's gospel: The paralytic walked home. Jairus' dead daughter lived. The woman who had been bleeding for twelve years stopped bleeding. Two blind men could see, and a mute who was demon possessed was released. These, and many more, were all totally healed. So why not me? It took me over twenty years to recover from ME (I'll leave Sue to speak about that in her chapter) and forty-five years to start being restored from child abuse.

Is it alright to ask the Lord these questions? I think so, because it's the only way we get answers. One answer is, 'You are not going to be perfect until you see Jesus'. I'm not impressed with that answer even though it is right.

May I suggest another answer? As we said earlier, Jesus Himself has scars. His wounds are healed. His scars will forever remind us of his victory, his triumph and his glory. Most important is that the Father planned and permitted this in the Son for high eternal reasons and our glorious good. We too, are permitted to have scars for a similar reason, '... for the display of his splendour' we read in Isaiah 61:3, and '... for the praise of his glory' in Ephesians1:12 and it is repeated in verse 14 '... to the praise of his glory.'[2]

Recall Paul's words about his thorn in the flesh as a messenger from Satan to torment him. It certainly feels like torment.[3] He pleads with God to take it away; and don't we do that? God's word to Paul was that grace is everything he needs and the divine power he needs is invested in human weakness. Can I comprehend this? God gives His grace in my torment and His power in my weakness. The pain, the torment, the embarrassment, has to be weighed against the greater benefit. My scars are displaying his grace and his power.

So, Julian of Norwich is right. God does not see them as blemishes but as honours. God doesn't see any defect in me, because he has done a miraculous work in me through the death of Christ. He sees me as 'holy in his sight, blameless and free from accusation.'[4] He awards me with these medals of honour so that others might have hope by seeing me wear God's glory.

I have always thought that those who shine the brightest have been polished up by past suffering. Perhaps I am being permitted to join them wearing medal scars. If so, like an old veteran, I need to wear them quietly. They are there, with all their meaningful colour and purposeful radiance.

They do not need much speaking about; just wearing for His glory. Battle worn and weary, scarred and weak, but displaying the glory of my Saviour's victory.

Why not wear scars like medals then? They are reminders of Jesus' victory, triumph and glory; they display His splendour; they bring Him praise and glory; they invest in me the grace and the power I so urgently need; and they are what my Father planned for the benefit of me—and of others also.

Chapter 9

Restoration, faith and bouncing between phases

'God whispers to us in health and prosperity, but, being hard of hearing, we fail to hear God's voice in both. Whereupon God turns up the amplifier by means of suffering. Then his voice booms.'

C.S. Lewis.

As a born and bred Yorkshireman, I enjoy rustic stone walls and always wanted to renovate an old building with oak beams. In 2005, we bought an old barn in the middle of France with a couple of dilapidated workman's cottages that had been used as hen houses. We decided to renovate these first. It was like a grimy hovel from a Dickens novel. The cottage roof leaked and was unstable which meant that the floors and some of the impressive beams were now rotten. The lath and plaster walls were threadbare. The windows, doors and what remained of staircases were ancient and the lime plaster walls were charred black from the open wood fires. All the plaster had to be hacked off the walls. What a colossal mess! But then, when the rubble had been cleared, new floors could be laid, fresh plaster spread on walls, and new stud walls put up so that a brand new design started to take shape. It is almost finished and certainly habitable. As a family, we have many happy memories on holiday even with all the blood, sweat and tears of renovation!

The journey of restoration is very similar to this. Where there is hope and some determination, a wrecked life over a long period can be gradually and painfully brought into a new phase of life. It is not an overnight transformation but a time-consuming restoration through the different stages. Some of us may eventually become a new stable home that is like a palace compared with what we were. The reality is that for most of us it is a never-ending journey with stops and starts, bounding forward one day and falling back the next. In it all, and overall, there is progress. But it cannot be done alone. This is where a Christian community is a place of healing. A place where upheavals are recognised as a normal part of the rebuilding process. Where the dream for a better future can come true.

Sue and I were at college a few years ago preparing to work abroad as missionaries. While we were there, Sue started to research the subject of human trafficking. She discovered a leading author on YouTube and then ordered her book from America. She read it, and suggested that I might like to look at it. As I read page after page, alarm bells started ringing and I found that I was no longer thinking about survivors in general but about me as a survivor.[1]

Judith Herman is associate clinical professor of psychiatry at the Harvard Medical School and has studied trauma in war veterans, rape victims and survivors of child abuse. She is also the Director of training at the Victims of Violence Program at Cambridge Hospital (USA). It is only relatively recently that Post-Traumatic Stress Disorder (PTSD) has become a recognised condition. Soldiers who survived the horrors of war returned home with disturbing symptoms that at first were dismissed but eventually became recognised for what they were—deep injuries to the emotions and the mind. These heroes were obviously changed by their traumatic experience. Similar patterns were seen in rape victims and survivors of child abuse. Precious lives have been cruelly distorted on the inside like a wrecked car, while presenting a variety of distracting cover-up paint jobs courageously on the outside.

Over the last ten years or so in the UK, we have seen the lid come off a vile can of snakes. We have heard of institutional sexual abuse, incestual abuse, organised paedophile rings and the trafficking of people for a monstrous and relentless sex industry.

Judith Herman lays out the long journey that is taken by survivors to gain some degree of restoration from a past trauma. We were no longer able to go abroad for financial reasons. We had left our church and our paid employment. We had nowhere to live and our furniture was stored in the middle of France. I had plenty of time to read. It was like waking up from a nightmare to find that the nightmare was real. It is not the people out there who I needed to facilitate a journey of restoration for. It was me, right here, that I needed to facilitate it for. In Gregory the Great's words, 'Preacher, heal thyself'.[2]

Chapter 9

There is one thing a survivor knows only too well. The journey ahead towers over us like an Everest Mountain and it is likely that we will never reach the summit in this life. What I needed to realise is the obvious fact that I could not do this alone. I would need people with me and professional help also. In the first instance, it was helpful to chat with a Christian psychotherapist and with doctors. It was important to assess the damage and acknowledge the seriousness of the restoration ahead. With the realisation of the vastness of the rebuilding work, and all the demolition needed before that could begin, came an overwhelming sense of helplessness. Accompanying this, like a flood, was my own powerlessness to change, the fear of whether our marriage would actually survive this, and whether, in the long haul, I could manage to persevere. This seemed like the ultimate impossibility on a par with raising the dead.

It is important to be realistic at this point, because it is here that we discover a turning point. I could not do it; I needed God to do a work. Only the architect and builder can restore my life. Ultimately Jesus, the Messiah can do this because this is what he was sent to do. A new challenge dawned on me. How big was my God? Was He just as big as this mountain or bigger? Was I making Him smaller than the world or did I genuinely believe that His world and everything in it is so small compared to Him. How big was my God? Did He send the second person of the Godhead to do this? My faith had to relax back into the armchair of all that God is. My Designer-Creator God is able to do this. He alone can raise the dead!

Phase one on a journey of Restoration: Safety and Security

'A broken heart is the only sound heart.'
John Trapp

'God is our refuge and strength, an ever present help in trouble.'
Psalm 46:1

Reading Judith Herman's research provoked this journey of restoration, while relying on God, keeping an open Bible and accepting advice from wise counsellors. It is this journey I outline for you here, not that this will necessarily be the journey you take. But I do hope that it will give you hope and courage to take your own steps to a degree of restoration. Please allow me to restate that this is a Christian layman's point of view and one personal journey. I do not know Judith Herman's religious beliefs, but I value her God-given wisdom. Chart 2, on the next page, sketches the phases of the journey.

This journey is no smooth highway; it is a rough road that bounces the traveller all over the place, and you are in the jeep! It is neither flat nor straight. Wonderfully though, the rough terrain will give way to flat, straighter tarmac roads as new routes and routines are established. There is hope, my journeying friend, there is hope!

As we begin the journey we need to be safe and secure. To follow my earlier analogy, before any work can be started on an old dilapidated building it must be made safe and the foundations secured. The work can be dangerous or disastrous without it. The mess of abandonment, distrust, helplessness, isolation and fear, needs to be made safe and given a solid environment. It is likely that there will be muddled questions of guilt, shame and blame clouding the truth: 'Was I to blame for this?' or 'Did I deserve

CHART 2 A Journey of Restoration - Jesus came here "to bind up the broken hearted"

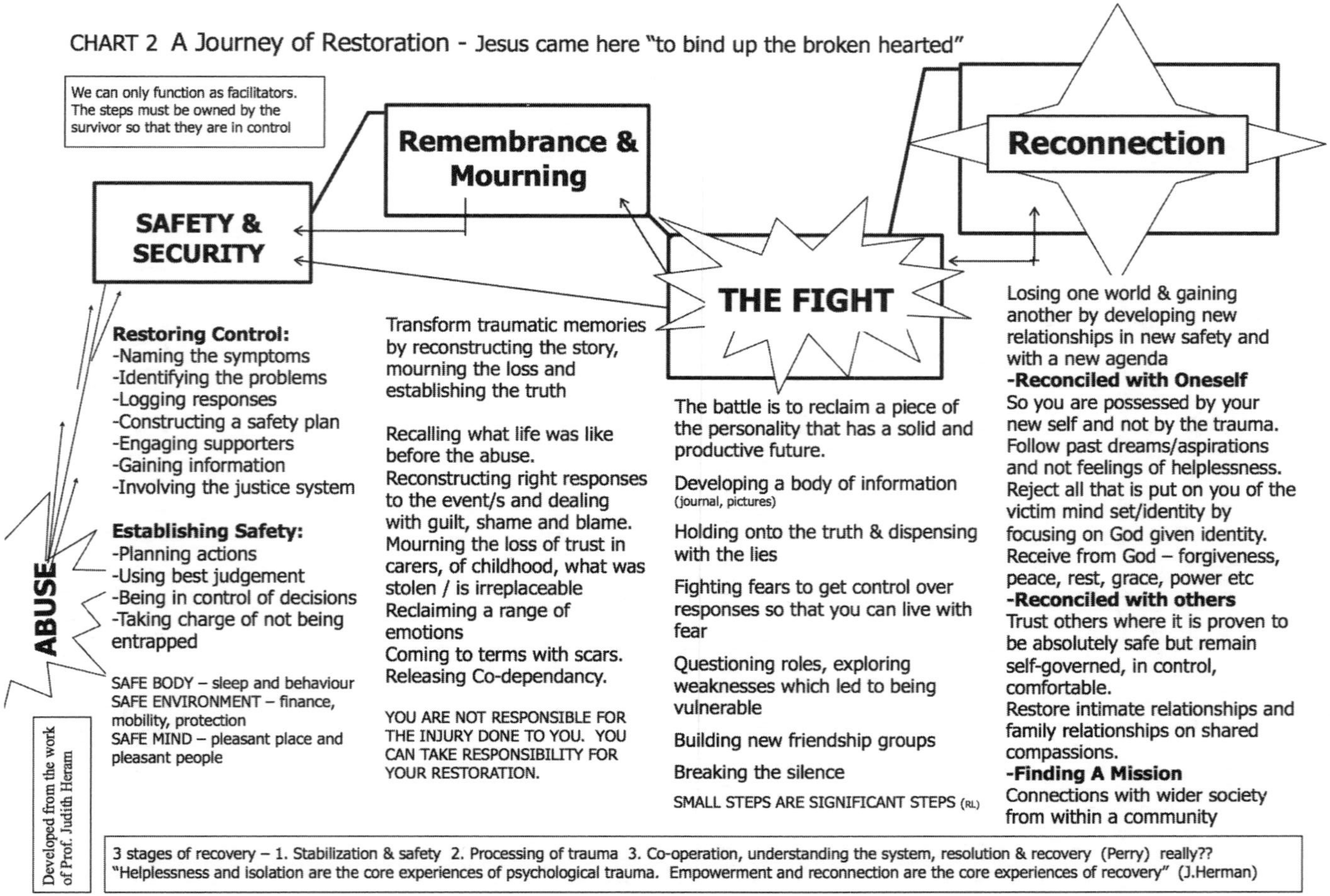

We can only function as facilitators. The steps must be owned by the survivor so that they are in control

ABUSE

Developed from the work of Prof. Judith Heram

SAFETY & SECURITY

Restoring Control:
-Naming the symptoms
-Identifying the problems
-Logging responses
-Constructing a safety plan
-Engaging supporters
-Gaining information
-Involving the justice system

Establishing Safety:
-Planning actions
-Using best judgement
-Being in control of decisions
-Taking charge of not being entrapped

SAFE BODY – sleep and behaviour
SAFE ENVIRONMENT – finance, mobility, protection
SAFE MIND – pleasant place and pleasant people

Remembrance & Mourning

Transform traumatic memories by reconstructing the story, mourning the loss and establishing the truth

Recalling what life was like before the abuse.
Reconstructing right responses to the event/s and dealing with guilt, shame and blame.
Mourning the loss of trust in carers, of childhood, what was stolen / is irreplaceable
Reclaiming a range of emotions
Coming to terms with scars.
Releasing Co-dependancy.

YOU ARE NOT RESPONSIBLE FOR THE INJURY DONE TO YOU. YOU CAN TAKE RESPONSIBILITY FOR YOUR RESTORATION.

THE FIGHT

The battle is to reclaim a piece of the personality that has a solid and productive future.

Developing a body of information (journal, pictures)

Holding onto the truth & dispensing with the lies

Fighting fears to get control over responses so that you can live with fear

Questioning roles, exploring weaknesses which led to being vulnerable

Building new friendship groups

Breaking the silence

SMALL STEPS ARE SIGNIFICANT STEPS (RL)

Reconnection

Losing one world & gaining another by developing new relationships in new safety and with a new agenda

-Reconciled with Oneself
So you are possessed by your new self and not by the trauma.
Follow past dreams/aspirations and not feelings of helplessness.
Reject all that is put on you of the victim mind set/identity by focusing on God given identity.
Receive from God – forgiveness, peace, rest, grace, power etc

-Reconciled with others
Trust others where it is proven to be absolutely safe but remain self-governed, in control, comfortable.
Restore intimate relationships and family relationships on shared compassions.

-Finding A Mission
Connections with wider society from within a community

3 stages of recovery – 1. Stabilization & safety 2. Processing of trauma 3. Co-operation, understanding the system, resolution & recovery (Perry) really??
"Helplessness and isolation are the core experiences of psychological trauma. Empowerment and reconnection are the core experiences of recovery" (J.Herman)

this?' or 'Could I have done more to avoid this?' and certainly, 'How can I speak to another person when I feel so ashamed?' Thoughts like these can hang over us and the restoration work like dark, threatening storm clouds.

For decades, I did not recognise the mess on the building site because I had grown accustomed to it, like Eskimos living under a dark sky for much of their year. The journey began in earnest as some of this clutter was removed, and this began by acknowledging the cause and God's perspective. Over the years, I had put in place some simple but invaluable structures. But now I found a strange but great liberty in naming the root problem. *This was child abuse.* It caused trauma which was underlying sleepless nights, amnesia and other difficulties (listed on the chart in chapter 6).

'Acknowledging the reality of the condition and taking steps to change are signs of strength not weakness; initiative not passivity.'[1] For reasons I do not understand, this 'acknowledging the reality' started to restore control which in turn created stability and safety. I began to write out truths on a piece of card and keep them in my pocket so I could read them regularly. My mind needed to hold onto what is true so that the dark clouds of lies could be pushed away.

Three nails in my thinking are the points from Psalm 139 mentioned in chapter 5.

- I am an awesome creation because God is an awesome Creator (v.13–15)
- I have been given a life which God has prepared and permitted in every part (16–18)
- I am secure and shaped by the hand of the Sovereign Lord God Almighty (1–12, 22–24)

I kept this in my pocket so that I could feed my thoughts on what God always says about me. It maintained a healthy balance between acknowledging what had happened to me and how God saw me. We need to remind ourselves that God our Father defines *who* we are and *what* we are, and *not* what has happened to us (nor what others think or say). I was determined to hold tightly to these statements of truth until they nailed in place safe ways of thinking.

Building this journey of restoration began when Sue and I were at college in 2012. We were on a three-month full-time training programme to prepare us for working abroad. In his first talk, the college director spoke to us about a safe, secure place and a spacious place that God provides for us. I realised that this was something God wanted me to experience constantly; after all it is a constant theme in the Bible.

Here it is again in Psalm 139. God knows us through and through, inside out. He knows where I go, what I think, when I rest, and He is acquainted with all I do. He even knows what I will say before I speak.[2] My heavenly Father is in the minute detail of my daily life as well as in the big events. His hand is in front going ahead of me and behind me guarding me. But his hand is also upon me. Just as I rest my hand on one of the grandchildren to reassure them, so his hand rests on me. The hand of the Sovereign Lord God almighty is round me and on me. No wonder David now says that he cannot get his head around this. It is so amazing that it is outside what any human mind can contain. I stopped praying for God's hand to be on me and instead started to thank him that it was.

God's hand is the ultimate place of safety and security. The destructive habits used to deaden the pain, needed to be exchanged for this. Alcohol or drugs are commonly used, but for me it was also the other more 'acceptable' forms of self-punishment or escapism like workaholism. Alcohol was one thing that I had relied on as a teenager and escaped into periodically. However, to maintain progress I needed to construct realistic alternatives to destructive habits. I found that having a safe place in my mind to go to was a significant help. There was an overgrown field just up the road from the school in Bradford where I was a child. That was my safe place, I used to lie on my back looking at the clouds in a blue sky on a warm day. Lying back in the surrounding hands of God Almighty was now my safe place.

Singing in the Cathedral was also a haven. Singing God's praises heartily puts me in God's hands. This is not just on Sundays. Whether alone in the house or in the car, I set my mind and heart after God. 'Since then you have been raised with Christ, set your hearts on things above, where Christ is seated at the right hand of God. Set your minds on things above, not on earthly things.'[3]

Knowing that as God's child it is impossible to get away from Him is a great security. Everywhere in the universe, to the furthest heavens or down to the deepest depths and everything in between, He is there. I can be up first thing in the morning or travelling abroad. and God is there directing and caring for me. Again, David is referring to the hand of God and the right hand of God—His ultimate sovereign power—leading and holding him. It doesn't matter if it is night or day, dark or light, he easily sees him.[4] What solid ground this is to be partnered with God in establishing safety and self-care.

I was establishing safety and security so that the building work would restore me and my life to what God intended. I kept coming back to this statement. God our Father defines *who* we are and *what* we are and *not* what has happened to us (nor what others think or say). Isn't it remarkable that we are God's masterpieces? God sculpted me in the studio of my mother's womb and I need to agree that he, as always, did a good job. He supervised all the work over that nine months and therefore it had to be to his standard.[5] He was preparing me to be his child by setting me apart (which is taken as the equivalent of 'wonderfully made' in the *English Standard Version* footnote). He saw me and loved me then in the darkness and the depths from when I was just a dot. Can I agree then that I am an awesome creation because God is an awesome Creator? Yes, I can, because I accept that my Maker defines *who* I am and *what* I am and *not* what had happened to me.

Safety plans were drawn up to apply this as practically as possible. This can be done with a supporter, but we should not fear asking for professional help. Those who need to get away from an abusive environment need to find a safe house or a refuge. Reading up-to-date research and the experience of others, often with a more severe experience than mine, was another safety factor. Knowledge does become power when it is a power of understanding which leads to action. For some survivors, there may come a time when restoring control may be through taking legal advice or going to court.

I drew strength from knowing that God had prepared my life before my mother thought about me. When I planned what I was going to do, and the steps I would take in establishing safety, it enhanced my well-being. I began to have occasional feelings of competence in the face of hopelessness. God had written down the journey of my life so I was free to live it from his hand to the best of my ability. By making some decisions, and they were not always the right ones, I gained a sense of freedom from what had held me and who had controlled me in the past. The fact that God has thought about me, designed and created me, holds me secure, guides me and more, is massive. These thoughts of his cannot be numbered and are so overwhelming that I fall asleep. When I wake up he is still the same and will not let me go.[6]

This place of safety is a great place to be. But there is a word of warning at this stage which Judith Herman gives. At this point, there can be a rapid recovery when control is restored but this is not recovery from the trauma. We need to continue on the journey beyond establishing an all-important safety. This is far more difficult for some survivors, and I appreciate this.

The security I had in God's hand was the foundation for stability in a number of areas. Stability came from

- a safe body: sleep control and dealing with destructive habits.
- a safe environment: self-protection, a safe place to live and organising finances or transport.
- a safe mind: making it a pleasant place with thoughts from 'pleasant' people and holding onto truth so that it governed my thinking.

One thing I did to develop a safe body was change habits. Alcohol was replaced with drinking long fizzy fruit drinks or eating nuts or chocolate. I found adjustments like these helpful. (Although I think chocolate has become a bit addictive so I have to calendar in periods of abstinence!). Creating a safe environment entails difficult choices and sacrifices. It may mean losing home, friends and livelihood. Child abuse survivors may lose their family.[7] We must tell ourselves: 'Do not bypass this stage, you have begun a marathon building task, endure, repeat, practice!'

This is a rough journey so accept there may be no giant leaps. Instead, be happy with small steps and the unfortunate slip-ups. Accepting that there will be failures along the way and getting into an environment where failure is acceptable is a great help. Remember, 'All musicians fail. All you can do is fail better.' By God's grace we should all be learning to fail better! Let's join the characters in the Bible who learned this lesson well. Someone unknown to me wrote, 'It is not what we do that defines who we are; what defines us is how well we rise after falling'. If you are trying to support someone and do not have this perspective, then you will be deeply disappointed when things do not go according to your plan.

You might be asking, 'Who can possibly assist me with this?' or 'Where are the compassionate individuals to support me during these times?' We need to be prepared to meet shock and horror from some people, including godly believers. There are some counsellors who are trained in trauma counselling, but this may be an expensive route. It may be that what is needed is a friend who will listen, love and empower you on the journey. This, of course, is risky because it involves trust.

Be aware that victims of trauma are not helped by well-meaning people who want to organise their life for them or dictate a road of recovery to them. At the least, it will shut them down and at worst it can re-traumatise them. Survivors have been controlled once before and will naturally recoil at any sniff of an authoritarian influence over them. The person who has learned to listen with their heart and to love unconditionally without judging, is a soothing ointment to a sore wound. This allows healing.

The survivor needs to take back control; the very thing that they have been robbed of. They need to be in the driving seat with God. A facilitator and not a director is what is needed. The facilitator provides an environment and some equipment but without any strings attached; no conditions, no expectations, not needing feedback, nor the buzz of fulfilment, and no expectation of 'thank you'. If there are steps of success these are the survivor's own property.

Although survivors have taken a huge step forward, it is likely that it is only tentative at this stage. This step of trust can be like going to the moon: 'Can I really trust this person, having been so badly let down by a trusted adult figure before?' Most of us put out a few 'feelers' to see how someone will respond. If they can be trusted, then we may reveal more. To take these big 'trust steps' they will have to overcome rampant feelings of abandonment and fears of being let down again. This safe environment is found in God; it can, and is, facilitated by genuine unconditional love. This points back to God and away from ourselves. An eighteen-year-old survivor put it this way after meeting some Christians.

'I could see that they loved me. I could feel it. It was in their faces and their words and in the kind things they did because God was with them for sure. They didn't do this to have something from me; they just did it.'

The ultimate place of safety and security is in God himself. The building site of our lives is made safe by taking to heart what God says about himself in relation to us and acknowledging where we are in his purposes. This is one of the Bible's reoccurring themes.[8]

In Psalm 139:14 we see that God knows us completely and this is for us to know. What has broken us doesn't need to lock us up in self-destruction. It can lead us to this safety and security in God where we discover opportunities for personal growth. Our broken heart in God's hands is a solid heart. God has already 'searched me'. I am solidly safe being searched, seen and led by Him.[9] In brokenness, we discover a depth of security, identity and mission in God we might never have known in any other way.

We can summarise phase one, our safety and security in the following ways:

- Knowing that our Father God knows us inside out and that we are his master piece.
- Acknowledging the cause of our trauma.
- Finding a safe place in God and living there in our mind.
- Developing this safety in our body, mind and environment.
- Gathering knowledge which leads to understanding and action.
- Restoring control.
- Accepting that small steps are significant steps and engaging with trusted supporters.

These are some of the ways we grow a personal safety and security. This is more than a crucial starting place it is a foundation as we continue our journey.[10]

Phase two on a journey of Restoration: Remembrance and Mourning

'When I heard these things, I sat down and wept. For some days I mourned and fasted and prayed before the God of heaven.'

Nehemiah 1:4

I have only faced the loss of two people who I was close to—my Grandparents. But I have taken part in many funerals and held the hands (literally and metaphorically) of those who are bereft or those who are dying. One thing I have learnt is that we often underestimate the power and the necessity of the grieving journey. Like the renovation work on a building, it strips us back to the basic structures of our life and prepares a way for reconstruction of fresh new possibilities.

Mourning can be traumatic but is a necessary part of the healing process. We have known a number of people, perhaps you have, who refuse to mourn. They may be part of the old 'stiff upper lip' brigade. There are others who do not stop mourning, and ten years later are still mourning as if it were yesterday. I cannot think that either of these experiences is healthy.

In the Bible I find that kings mourn as do cupbearers,[1] highly successful individuals like Job or Joseph[2] and whole communities.[3] Jesus himself wept at the graveside of his friend Lazarus.[4] Andreas Kostenberger comments on this: 'Jesus' example shows that heartfelt mourning in the face of death does not indicate lack of faith but honest sorrow at the reality of suffering and death.'[5] As we grieve, we do so with hope set on our future with God and it is in our grieving that we find ourselves being comforted by God.

Nehemiah became one of God's great builders. He listened to the insights from others who knew the situation better than he did. His brother told him that the walls of Jerusalem were now broken down and the gates burnt. This gave him a burden that dominated all his usual commitments.[6] His mourning over this tragic situation propelled him into prayer and a deeper devotion to God; then into courageous action. It was this devotion to God that sustained him then, and in the future. He looked for a chance to get permission from the king, to take time off to build. It was a great risk for him to look glum in the presence of his king but he had a cause worth dying for. His prayer is one of the great prayers of the Bible. His actions were one of the heroic and significant faith missions with God.[7]

Where did Nehemiah's amazing work begin? It began with a realisation that something that belonged to God had been broken down, and that brought him to tears. He mourned over the disgrace of his own people and the trouble they were in after an attack that destroyed their defences and deeply affected the way they lived. Shouldn't the survivor learn to mourn for the same reasons and in a similar way? The secret disgrace, the unspoken trouble and the destructive effect on their life should be brought into the light, grieved over and dealt with. Tamar grieved immediately over what was done to her.[8] Nehemiah was grieving after the walls had been down for some sixty or seventy years.[9] The grief that adds to the mourning is that for some survivors, like me, it takes decades before the journey begins. I was determined to find a healthy way to mourn and do so in a way that would lead to constructive actions.

When I recognised the impact of child abuse on my life, I decided to treat it (not the people) as the enemy and go to war against it. What I told myself was, 'This tragic experience is an enemy which I am going to fight and win. I can then reclaim a damaged piece of my personality that has a solid and productive future. But I must try to do this without being re-traumatised.' Now the way I was to actually fight this battle was yet another surprise. An important part was healthy mourning. It was necessary to identify all the emotional states, the facts, the reasons, the guilt, and all the other excrement (sorry it needs to be called that) and move on. This is called, 'the reconstruction of the story' and it allows us to pass through mourning as a healthy experience.

In the early stages when we worked on our cottage in France, there were piles of old plaster and rotten timber that needed clearing out of the way. It was rubble that needed dumping. Once this was done, it left the whole environment looking coldly bare but ready for construction. Healthy mourning can clear out the rubble ready for restoration.

Some people need to revisit their life before the abuse and relish the ideals and dreams at that time. This can help us come to terms with what happened. I also found that retelling the events with the feelings and thoughts, let me establish the facts, emotional states, reasons, responsibility etc. In doing this I had to take great care to have a right view of myself in God. All the work from Psalm 139 on God's perspective was invaluable. The importance of this phase is to build dignity and value. It is the opposite of humiliation and shame. God lifts us up from a pit into his hand. Why, in my thinking, do I put myself back down there? Remember, we mourn and grieve so that we can move on. It is a vital part of the building work. 'When the act of telling the story is concluded the traumatic experience belongs in the past.'[10]

Important steps in renovating a building cannot be bypassed or rushed. A shoddy and even unsafe house would be the result. Coming to terms with the emotional damage and all the painful mess of re-occurring feelings needs to move us forward steadily so we take control. What is happening here? The heart cries out for someone to be the protector, the comforter, the trusted companion, as if demanding that someone should take the place of a father or mother. Could this be a reason why many victims of abuse go back into abusive relationships?

The only one who can realistically take control of my life is me. I cannot expect, and I certainly must not expect, anyone else to take that place. It only spells disaster. Now for me, God is my protector, comforter and trusted companion. Words which, if I do not take care, can slide through my mind without any grip on my life. The unconditional, all-powerful, eternal love of my Father in heaven is the best place and the safest place for me to grieve. Oh, to know His love in all its dimensions.[11] Like Nehemiah, it is with God I build to honour his name. I look to him for success and direction and enjoy his hand upon me.[12]

One of the first things Nehemiah did when he arrived on site was to make a careful assessment. He did this without letting anyone know what his mission from the Lord was. He examined the walls carefully and privately, even though there was rubble in the way.[13] The work then began with others who had been neglecting the walls for some sixty or seventy years. Perhaps they couldn't face it because it was such a massive job. Or was it that they had been busy with other things. All it took was for a leader to point out the need and the work began; and it involved the entire community.[14]

As I assessed the damage in my life I could see three facts that became painful healing encounters.

1. I was not responsible for the injury to me as a boy.

Just like Nehemiah was not responsible for broken down walls nor Tamar when she was raped. I may have been unwise, or gullible, or even made some foolish decisions, but that is the nature of a young boy. It was vital that I accepted that these were child molesters, pedophiles or perpetrators who sinned against me. It was their sin and not mine. Of course, we can mourn for our own sin against God. But in addition to grieving over personal sin or the wrong that we have done, we can mourn the wrong that has been done to us.[15]

2. I am not responsible for being abandoned.

For me, being left at boarding school was like being put into care. I wanted to sing in the cathedral but I did not want to be separated from my family. I did not choose to be in a position of vulnerability, unprotected from the selfish desires of predators.

3. I am responsible for my own journey of restoration.

We are not responsible for the injury done to us, nor for being put in a place of vulnerability, but we can take responsibility and be proactive in our recovery. We can be builders. No one else can do it for me, although restoration does involve the help of others. Getting this cleared up is a significant step forward. But I find that I still need to remind myself of these three facts.

Clearing this rubble out of the way makes room for constructive renovation work to begin. How can this be done efficiently and effectively so that it can be dumped decisively and effectively?

When Nehemiah realised what had happened, he 'sat down and wept.' He records that, 'For some days I mourned and fasted and prayed before the God of heaven.'[16] We cannot tell exactly how many days he did this for. But he did not pass through this in an afternoon or an evening. It was for 'some days' and these days he spent with God fasting and praying. No one knew about this. It was between him and God. This was a deeply significant time that shaped his future.

What we are allowed to see in his mourning is that he has a *right view of God* (his awesomeness, faithfulness and love), and he is in a *right place before God* (he is stripped back to know the depth of sinfulness). Nehemiah refers to God's word and his promises (reflecting on the reasons for the great loss of these walls); and he respectfully intercedes for others and himself.[17] In the first half of his prayer he grieves over this great loss; in the second half, he pleads a case for the success of his mission. As he mourns, fasts and prays in these two areas, he shows a deep devotion to God which then leads into courageous action.

In God's hand, my safe place, I could constructively remember and mourn. With a right view of God's awesomeness, faithfulness and love to me (see previous chapter) I can safely grieve the loss and plead a case. I should do this as Nehemiah did, recognising that someone who belonged to God had been 'broken into' causing the secret disgrace, the unspoken trouble and the destructive effects. The healthy way to do this was to grieve the loss with a right view of God and be in a right place before God acknowledging the depths of sinfulness that was involved. How would I do this significantly so that it builds a productive future?

I should grieve the loss as if I were grieving the death of a close friend.

Whenever I spoke to people about going off to boarding school I would recall the tearful goodbyes. Even as a big thirteen-year-old, who had graduated into his grey flannel long trousers, I choked back the tears on my mother's shoulder. The boy quite naturally wanted his mother's company and comfort. It was as simple as that. In all of us there is a deep emotional craving to be wanted, appreciated and needed. This was clearly one of the reasons I was drawn to Sue because our relationship pacified the feeling of abandonment. When, for some reason, I believed that Sue was rejecting me, the feelings of abandonment were overwhelming. All my life I had tried to bypass these emotions (we look at this in a later chapter). Now, I needed to grieve the loss of time with my mother and family, the onset of abandonment and rejection, and the introduction of other destructive factors such as compensating with fantasy or substance abuse. These were easy to recall. But a number of connected losses were far more subtle, taking time to surface.

I had lost the foundation of a basic trust and belief in good parents, responsible teachers and carers. A natural trust and belief in adults was stolen. There was the loss of life down the decades while the lid was kept on the disgrace, trouble and destructive effects. The significant effect on our marriage meant that there was a loss of general intimacy. There was an impact on my childhood because it was kept a secret. I had lost a childhood freshness, an openness to react as I explored life. I would call this the loss of freedom since that time. All of this was not dealt with as a child; I did not have the support to deal with it. Therefore, a part of my childhood was stolen and is now irreplaceable. Yet at that time there was a definite sense, when I was in the cathedral, that God was my Father. In grieving, I recognise the depth of sin by those who abused me, but also that God was there for me. I prayed that the Lord would show me how to grieve this loss in a healthy way and truly grieve—but without self-indulgence.[18]

I should claim back the emotions of my loss and the emotions of my freedom.

Like Nehemiah I could plead a case on the promises of God. Doesn't God say to his devastated people that he will restore the years that the locusts have eaten?[19] He does that by letting us know his presence with us as it is he alone who restores our soul.

When all is stripped away what do you have left? What is ground zero like when everything has gone? This is a question I asked myself at the time. At this point of the journey I had Jesus, no job, no home, no church, and little self-confidence. But I had Jesus. All was stripped away, and I did not like it. The only choice I faced, as far as I could see, was to start from scratch or run away. My heart knew that Jesus would only approve of the first. So, this is what ground zero is like! Nehemiah found that this was the right place to be before God. It is crucial to be in his presence and to know his presence.

At this stage, God-given wholesome desires for companionship and meaningful relationships needed to be in the light.[20] The damage done to these desires by a predator should be brought into the light. The harm that these damaged desires have done to others needs also to be laid open. Emotions that have never changed. They have not been acknowledged, or addressed, or understood. But they are being given an airing in the light of Jesus now. All the busyness of life has been a welcome method of locking them down, quite conveniently most of the time. The 'Light of the world' (Jesus), has shone into this dungeon and there have been steps out in response. This surely is included in what is meant by walking in the light. My whole approach was to keep it a secret in order not to tarnish my parents' reputation, and for me, to avoid the pain of shame. Therefore, the lid stayed on the can.

As a follower of Christ who wants to grow spiritually I have denied myself, which I understood to include denying self-centred emotions. Does the Lord want us to deny our need for love and companionship? In His eyes, is this desire self-centred or is it the way God has made us? We are to take off lust, greed, jealousy, bitterness and other deceitful desires like we would dirty clothes. Would we include with those emotions our basic desire to be loved? There is a clear distinction between what is pure and impure, wholesome and unwholesome, godly and ungodly. (e.g. Ephesians 4:31–32, Galatians 5:19–23). Surely the Lord, who lived in intimate fellowship with his Father, would have shown us how He denied himself that loving fellowship if he intended for us to deny it. There was only one occasion when He did, and that was when He took the sin of the world on himself. In that exceptional moment, the Lord Jesus was cut off from his Father.[21]

On the journey of transformation, we can discover the unfathomable love of God in our times of pain and suffering. The pressure of suffering develops perseverance. Over time this leads to a proven character and then on to a certain hope of our future with God. All this is qualified and supported by God's mighty love soaking through us.[22] As God's children we no longer live under the dictatorship of our old counterproductive nature. We are now to live by the gracious governing of the Holy Spirit who grows in us his fruit. This fruit includes emotion but it grows mainly in the soil of our will and actions as part of a God-like character. The Lord is growing in us His: 'love, joy, peace, patience, kindness, goodness, faithfulness, gentleness and self-control.'[23] Shouldn't we be delighting in this and plead our case for the Lord to restore this? Shouldn't we also be pleading a case for others?

This is a point Judith Herman makes. We should claim the right to feel a full range of emotions as an act of resistance to the perpetrator. Not as an act of revenge but as an act of resistance, because we are not to be tied in any way to them. The walls would be built up again. I wanted to have the full range of emotions so that I had the capacity genuinely to love everyone, even my perpetrators. Why should I not have peace, joy and love in good measure? For me this seemed a reasonable step; it was choosing to love my enemy.

Mourning is a process we pass through by accepting that the only thing that we are truly responsible for is our own recovery; and by healthy grieving and by claiming back emotions we move, significantly, towards wholeness. This takes time, as does seeing the Lord in it with us. He is the One who binds up the broken hearted.[24] What makes this an even greater challenge is that we may have to work through this alone or even when we have misunderstandings with those we love. Here, we are most like Nehemiah, who began alone with God.

A healthy approach to remembrance and mourning helps to close the past and go forward. We grieve the loss of childhood freshness and openness, of trust and belief in responsible carers, and of the support and safeguarding that was needed at the time. We gradually claim back the emotions which were lost and as a full range of emotions that we can have today. Although we move on from grieving we do return here on our journey from time to time. But here is another question to consider: Is it possible to improve our condition?

Phase three on a journey of Restoration: The fight for a Sound Mind and a Productive Life

> 'I sit here like a fool and hardened in leisure, pray little, do not sigh for the church of God, yet burn in a big fire of my untamed body. In short, I should be ardent in spirit, but I am ardent in the flesh, in lust, laziness, leisure, and sleepiness ... Already eight days have passed in which I have written nothing, in which I have not prayed or studied; this is partly because of temptations of the flesh, partly because I am tortured by other burdens.'
>
> Martin Luther[1]

One survivor my wife and I see regularly has a great expression. 'It's mad!' She sees the powerful dynamics of a truth and says, 'It's mad!' Discovering the love of God and rediscovering it, is a most powerful factor for radical change in our experience. Another aspect of God's character, that has a transforming power, is his Holiness and our pleasure from purity. Now this is a double 'mad'. When the Lord led His people back from captivity he gave them an open highroad which he called 'the Highway of Holiness'.[2] They did not have to strive to get up onto this open road. They were put there.

I have often been struggling to become something for God that He has already made me to be. Although I know I have a responsibility to grow in godliness, I tend to forget about the holy purity that Jesus has clothed me with. He gives me a powerful taste for purity.

Now this is the really 'mad' bit. This pleasure from purity isn't something we pursue, although it is good to. It is something which overtakes us. At the end of their journey 'Gladness and joy will overtake them.'[3] Heaven with this, and much more, is ahead. Now that we have been born from heaven we have some of this overtaking joy now in the pleasure of purity. We can look down on the enemy, and every temptation, from the position of our pleasure in purity. This is what God planned for us and what Jesus has achieved. Shame and disgrace are to be lifted away and replaced with joy in an inheritance twice the size that we could expect.[4]

What I marvel at in all this, is that what God works in us to give Himself the most pleasure, gives us the most pleasure. New emotions breed in the daily mental hygiene He provides and I maintain.

Once safety in our security has been established and a degree of mourning has been entered into, it is vital to realise ground can and should be taken back. We can fight back. This is another major step forward and the fight, like all the phases, needs to be returned to through all the ups and downs of the journey.

The sixteenth-century reformer Martin Luther had many 'downs' in which he appears to give up. Above is an extract he wrote to his friend Philip Melanchthon during such a time. The best of us struggle to 'fight the good fight'. But we ought to encourage each other, as often as we can, to fight on.[5]

To get an overview of what my alternatives were, I pictured them as a fight in the boxing ring. On a daily basis, I confronted the challenges of ravaging emotions that would lead in different directions. The centre of the ring was best, rather than being pushed onto the ropes at either extreme. At one end is self-indulgence and self-pity. At the other end are the downhill lows; the genuine emotions of self-destruction that can flood in unexpectedly.

OVERWHELMING EMOTIONS Self-destruction Booze, Escapism	**DETERMINED WILL, COMMITMENT** Self-control Prayer, Praise & Whole Truth Healthy Thoughts	**ROUTINE EMOTIONS** Self-indulgence or Self-pity Danger, Risk-taking

I began to see that my fight for a better life in the centre was worth fighting for. To fight my way there, I had to come off the ropes of fear and doubt in the face of bizarre emotional threats or plain routine emotions. This still involves standing my ground against the emotion and not running away from it. Running away is an impossibility of course. Even though you might escape from the person, the emotion goes with you. It might be the fear of being controlled again or a fear of abandonment or feelings of loneliness. Once we have tasted the power of God's love, the transformation begins. It helps us to grow a courageous determination not to be controlled again. This fresh sweet sense of solid and secure ground inspires us to keep away from the ropes of self-destruction.

The fight is never-ending. It is a daily battle to stand centre away from the edges. To this day I experience feelings of rejection because I still catch myself thinking that I am different. I therefore find it a challenge to meet up with a particular group of ministers because, even though I have known them for a long time, they seem to convey nonacceptance; it is as if I have been assessed and found wanting because I do not fit the mould, the norms of that group. Perhaps it is my imagination, but I do ask myself: 'Is there some truth to my thoughts?' On the other hand, I have few problems relating to a large group of ministers that meet up in Derbyshire every year because they are accepting. These feelings of nonacceptance, because of being different, are a classic struggle for survivors. How do we get to stand on that central ground?

The fight for a sound mind

I find that in the Bible, God has created the way for us to stand upright against any attack, and to stay standing when it has passed. In Ephesians 6 Paul shows us that this is like a Roman soldier's armour. The strongest defence for our minds are the great truths of the gospel, the helmet of salvation. Here, we hold on to what the Lord has done and won as a 'done deal' for every one of his people. This includes our perfect standing and safety from eternal death because sins have been forgiven. They are gone because He personally took them and God's anger against them when he died as our substitute on the cross. This convinces us of his unconditional love, and his resurrection brings to us his abundant life in the Holy Spirit.

It is also a fight to move forward and to see the Lord advancing his kingdom through us. I can do this by actively trusting in the *truth* instead of believing lies and see this hold everything in place (like a belt around my waist) so that I am free to run instead of stumble. The Lord's own *righteousness* (his gift of standing right and acceptable in God's holy presence) protects our heart and central organs. It protects all that he has gained as our way to live. His *peace-shoes* that I have from believing the good news of his triumph on the cross means that I can hold my ground and not back down. My puny faith is transformed into a large deflector *shield of faith* (when it looks to Jesus and is trusting in the solid ground of truth). This protects against any fiery missile and is a wall of iron that can push forward.[6] This is God's design so that we can stand on that central ground. How can I stand on that ground more of the time?

Tackling the thoughts and fighting in full armour to establish a new pathway of right thinking is what is important. How can a new pathway of thinking be established? By fighting for new ground in my mind and fighting off the old thoughts. I devised three cards from a discovery I made when I had ME so that I could practice this.[7]

1. Right now.

This is what I will think. My Father God is far bigger than any thought or person in authority. He has given me this great salvation, his righteousness, his cross etc. I am in his plan[8] and every day he has planned for me.[9] He is working all things together for my good.[10] He has made me to be his child.[11] He accepts me just as I am in Christ.[12] This is the reality right now and it is important for me to think like this—right now.

2. Stop.

I will not go that way in my thoughts. I reject that negative, destructive thought. I am not going to tread that path anymore. If that thought persists, I will take it as a captive to Jesus.[13]

3. Right thoughts.

This is the new pathway. I tell myself: 'You stand strong in all that Jesus is and has done which is transferred to you in the full armour. Think about wearing each piece and stand in the strength of each piece. Stand on other right thoughts. For example: you *are* different and that is the way God has made you to be. He has made you different for His purpose and to do something that others cannot do.[14] When you suffer in Christ your sacrifice is an aroma of Christ to God and to those around you.[15] So, fill the new thought-pathway with what is true, dignifying, right, pure, lovely, admirable, excellent and can be praised.[16]

What a battle this is, but it is worth it to be standing on the central ground. Sometimes we cannot do anything about the feelings, but the thoughts can be arrested and taken to our Lord who is the judge in the highest court. When thoughts (or feelings) persist, we can pray continuously (under our breath); often it's the best way to spend a sleepless night. They need to be taken to the blood-soaked cross-grave of Jesus and buried there and, perhaps also, shared with a trusted prayer partner. I try to remember that the real issue is not with people (it's tempting to think it is) but with spiritual forces who fight to have some control over us.[17] To return to the boxing analogy, if we keep our gloves up we protect ourselves against hits on our minds, our emotions, and our lives.

The battle for the truth

We can look forward to our transformation by new ways of thinking. The whole truth where we stand secure is not a rehearsal or a fantasy reenactment but a real fight. It is a battle for the way we think, where we stand and how we live. This armour, the battle equipment with which we dress ourselves, cannot be separated from the Lord's own character which he is growing in us. He promises that if we will dress up in him and stand in him 'strong in the Lord and in his mighty power' we will 'be able to stand (our) ground.'[18] This means that if I will stick with him there is no retreating. There is only a standing solid in that central ground.

So, there is the theory. What more can we do to get this into practice? One or two approaches have already been mentioned. Writing cards based on Scriptures and living them out in the day, is one practical way to fight back. Jesus took truth into his actions as part of his fight. He gives to us the Sword of the Spirit. What use is a sword if it is kept in its scabbard; and we don't want to think about what happens if I don't bother wearing a belt!

If Jesus needed truth to fight off the evil suggestions of the devil in the wilderness, then so do I. He made it quite clear that we were not to live only by the food that goes into our mouths but his word that has come out of God's mouth.[19] But, of course, it is not a matter of blandly quoting

Scripture. The Lord knew his own words, their purpose and their meaning, therefore he was not using them as a lucky charm to ward off evil, but as God's own word which cuts deeper into any situation like a warrior's blade.[20]

Of course, truth must be used in the way God designed it to be used. A sword in the wrong hands can be dangerous if slashed aimlessly in the air. God has designed it to be used by the Holy Spirit with his own spiritual expression. In this sense, God the Holy Spirit is teaching us as we read, as we hear and as we apply it. And how deeply harmful truth can be without grace or love.

The best way to practice truth is to get to know what it really says and then do what it says. Building up your own self-confidence is one thing. Building confidence in what God says about you (and in who God is and in what He does) is quite another thing. Beginning with what God says about us in Psalm 139 is his eternal truth about what he has done in us. His truth does not change when things change, or when our mood changes. Being thankful to God for his truth is another sure way of fighting back. We are told to count our blessings; giving thanks is a command.[21]

We know there are going to be challenging times. Our struggles could be as tough as Martin Luther's. How do we fight when we feel defeated or when we have failed? When there is the pain of isolation or when the old feelings of abandonment have sneaked up on us? One answer to this is to keep balanced thoughts so that we are ready for these times. These feelings are real, and behind them they have an experience of trauma. The battles are won or lost on the battlefield of our mind. How I think at these times will either push me overboard into a tsunami of emotions or, in time, bring me into control so that I stand in the centre and overcome them. Bad thoughts and bad feelings can sometimes come out of the blue. It is crucial to be realistic. I must not be too hard on myself but neither can I let myself go. There is a central ground where I develop a determined will and commitment.

Please be aware that it might be perfectly right to be angry. I have been with people when this has happened: a brother and sister who were made by their father to have sex together, or a child who dreaded the thought of her stepdad coming home because she knew that she would be raped again. When you have had a flashback to a moment of horror like this, your mind, which up until now has blanked the experience, will make you feel angry or grieved or have overwhelming questions: 'Why did God allow this to happen?'

Facing the demons of the past helps us to stand against bad thoughts in the present. There are many precious memories from my days as a student minister. One day I had a time of feedback with my mentor, Stanley Jebb, who was the senior pastor and Principal of the Ministry Training Institute. I sat in front of his office desk, overcome by realising what the job involved and particularly what I thought was the character of a church minister, and said, 'I think that you have the wrong man. If you knew my past you would not let me be a minister.' What Stanley said then had a profound impact on me, 'It is just that which means you will be able to reach people that I cannot reach.'

This simple fact was a revelation to me and it helped me to undo my wrong thinking. It is about God's faithfulness. It is not about what has happened to me or what I have done in the past. What is of highest importance is to leave with Him what He, in His eternal wisdom, has allowed. Much of that I don't understand and perhaps never will down here. But I give him his right to be God. He is faithful. All I could see, sitting with my mentor that day, was the blemishes of my past. I would look at all the other leaders in the church as people that had just had afternoon tea with the Archangel Gabriel. They were much further on and much better than me because they didn't have my chequered past. A right view of God and what He has done will lead to a realistic view of ourselves. A realistic and balanced view meant I could stand in that central ground.

We can eventually face our demons from the past and we should not fear the big questions. God is big enough to handle them especially when we do not have the answers. The demons of our past are the vivid thoughts of what was done to us that plague us, or the unwelcome and uninvited feelings. What has been done to us is evil and can only have been planned in hell to be the selfish destructive actions of a man or a woman against a child. That does not mean that we are evil or that we are possessed. I have never found this to be the case in a survivor.

Chapter 13

Phase four on a journey of Restoration and Reconnection

'Happiness is reconciliation with an old friend.'

Anon

'Emphasise reconciliation not resolution. It is unrealistic to expect everyone to agree about everything. Reconciliation focuses on the relationship, while resolution focuses on the problem. When we focus on reconciliation, the problem loses significance and often becomes irrelevant.'

Rich Warren.

Reconnecting, challenges us to keep relationships healthy. It can be hard for survivors to keep close relationships going. All those issues of rejection, trust, dependence, emotional sensitivity, and much, much more (that we listed in chapter 8 'What is it Really Like?') are the demon-monsters which keep us away or push others away. It is by far the easiest thing just to retreat into a defensive shell. But although that is powerfully attractive in a moment of time, it isn't the best option. Survivors, like everyone else, need to build interpersonal relationships. Reconnection is a challenge to renew and maintain healthy relationships. But during downtimes, when our feelings are raw and our defences are up, building relationships is a gigantic struggle.

We cannot miss this need for reconnection or reconciliation because it is repeated so many times in the Bible. Healthy relationships are at the heart of our life with God and making reconnections keeps relationships healthy.[1] Two ladies, Euodia and Syntyche, who had been part of a team working alongside Paul, had fallen out and it was affecting their effectiveness.[2] Paul begged them get together and harmonize in the Lord. The ESV footnote is interesting, commenting on Philippians 2:2 'be like minded':

'This does not imply a dry intellectual unity, rather, the Philippians are to use their diverse gifts in an agreeable, cooperative spirit, with a focus on the glory of God.'[3]

That is a strikingly positive way to see it. I knew that my relationships could benefit from being 'likeminded' in that way. Euodia and Syntyche needed to reconnect. The future of their team's effectiveness depended on it. This is what we explore in this chapter.

Another helpful outline is given in Ephesians 4 right in the middle of Paul's instructions to live in 'true righteousness and holiness' (by putting on the new self and putting off the old self). Paul lists some essentials: Stop 'bad mouthing' and instead say what builds people up and is beneficial. 'Get rid' of reactions like 'bitterness, anger and slander' but instead 'be kind, compassionate and forgiving'.[4] Our new life in Christ is about living like Christ. We do not do this as slaves to earn something but as children in the family mould and dearly loved. Because we are loved so greatly we now 'live a life of love'. We copy His supreme act of love in giving Himself up 'as a fragrant offering and sacrifice to God'.[5] That is to the point and a fine ideal. But how do we get near it?

Once the lid was off I acknowledged my past abuse and recognised its vile monstrous effects, but this left me emotionally raw. Security had been established. There had been times of grieving. Now that I could fight back, ground was being taken little by little but I was over-sensitive. Harsh words slipped out of my mouth almost on a daily basis. These brief moments were telling. They showed me I had resentment that had not been dealt with. What I think I resented was that I was still living as a victim. I acknowledged what had happened in the past and wanted to leave it there. I desperately wanted to move on into more healthy relationships.

Reconnection for Recovery

In the early stages of the journey of restoration, it seemed that I was being punished for what had happened. What is in the mind of a survivor is worked out in the nearest and dearest relationships. All I could do was pray for a heart of forgiveness. Meaningful relationships were being made in a new church we were attending, and this helped. But it would be many months before our relationships in our family could be re-established.

Serious wounds take serious time to heal. It is those 'who wait for the Lord (who) shall renew their strength; they shall mount up on the wings like eagles; they shall run and not be weary; they shall walk and not faint.'[6] I have found this promise to be a deep encouragement over the years. Relationships would one day be reconnected. For now, I must be sure to wait on the Lord to be connected to him.

This journey of reconnecting—by developing new relationships and renewing key relationships—is what Judith Herman describes as losing one world and gaining a new one:

'Helplessness and isolation are the core experiences of psychological trauma. Empowerment and reconnection are the core experiences of recovery.'[7]

It is in the new world we gain more control over emotions and responses by the grace we find there and not by simple formulas. Let's try to be realistic. Losing one world and gaining a new one does take time. I remember that being patient was not very attractive! But neither was cynicism.

Wise choices at this stage helped reconnection. I wanted to fight so that I did not become cynical, hardhearted and bitter, or even shut down on the inside. No, even in the pain, I wanted to laugh, have fun, express loving concern and generally be light instead of heavy, involved instead of distant. I was not willing to chug on like a car spluttering, unable to get out of first gear. Resting in what God was doing took me from helplessness and isolation to empowerment and reconnection. Keeping a focus on what he is doing now and not on what might happen in the future was a positively healthy way to think. Those who 'wait, will' is the promise. Paul had learnt that lesson well. This was a major step in living a life of love.

A deepening dependency on the Lord was not a conscious choice but natural necessity. It was also the only option, as I could not rely on other people, because it was not right to. I alone am responsible for handling my tsunami and I found that this could only be done with the Lord. I thank God for these breakthroughs. These are amazing times of stark revelation when the Lord connects us to a truth; we have a fresh and vibrant understanding; walls which barred us from hope are down; and there is a release into a land of a new-found liberty. We call these Jericho-wall-moments.

Let me give you an example of this. I have always deeply appreciated that God's own people are hidden in Christ. In that remarkable letter to the Ephesians the Christian's place 'in Christ' is underscored for us some fifteen times in the first chapter. This is how we live a life of love. To seal this in our thinking, in Colossians we are given the image of a double grip from the Trinity: 'You are hidden *in* Christ *in* God.'[8] The flipside of that is equally important and yet I had not fully grasped it, so my appreciation was somewhat shallow. The risen Lord Jesus Christ in the form of the Holy Spirit has taken up His home in me. This is an awesome wonder. The spiritually born child of God is seen by all of heaven to be a living temple area equivalent to the Holy of Holies in the temple in Jerusalem. A weak, broken human form like mine is a prized container of God's glory! 'Do you not know that your body is a temple of the Holy Spirit within you, whom you have from God?'[9] Jesus prayed as the basis of our unity, 'I have given them the glory that you gave me.'[10] All of this is the Father's answer to our Lord's prayer. I can trust my life on this and revel in it just as much as I marvel at it. It is here in Christ I can live a life of love and make reconnections.

Now this truth was of gigantic significance and therefore had a huge impact on my thinking and living. Why is such a spectacular emphasis needed here? Because I was living by admiring the promised land of this truth at a distance. Of course, I knew these things in my mind and savoured an intellectual appreciation of them. But where was the real experience and enjoyment of them in the rough and tumble of everyday living? It was the other side of the walls. It was during a time of fighting with lies and waiting on the Lord that this wall came down and reconnections were made.

A major Jericho-wall-experience was already behind me in discovering the root cause of many challenges and weaknesses. More land had to be taken; there were more walls the Lord needed to flatten. The revelation of Christ's holy presence, without reservation, being resident in me was overpowering. A profound joy was now released in me replacing the sorrow and anguish. How crucial it is to be strong enough to come out from behind our walls. The subtle walls of indifference, ignorance, superiority, judgementalism, fear, etc. which hold us back from knowing God's glory and keep us out of true unity.

Chapter 13

Renewing key relationships

'A new day is dawning' is a phrase that Sue and I started to use. We sensed in our spirits that the Lord was doing something new or bringing us into a new phase. We started to see encouraging changes in our church, in our family and in ourselves.

Thomas the tank engine and the other engines are directed by a stationmaster called the Fat Controller. When I think about the part of me that is directive and controlling, the Fat Controller comes to mind. He is quite sweet and very bossy, but the Fat Controller in us can have a more sinister edge. He (or she) has to control others. Once more we must face up to this on the journey of reconnection. Our old relationship is waving goodbye and we will welcome a new one. There is the loss of one world and the gaining of a new one. Under the management of Jesus, our commander-in-chief, we will be responsible for ourselves and not be looking to control others nor be controlled by others. This brought major changes in the way I related to other people. Sue began a new phase of independence.

Meeting up with my brother, who had similar experiences as a child, was my first step in renewing relationships on the journey of restoration. Reconnecting in relationships is important. Our relationship had been easy going but not exactly very close. When we met for lunch we found that we had much in common.

My Mum and Dad were due to come and see us. Up until now I didn't have peace about talking to them about the past; although it had been mentioned briefly a long time ago, so that they knew abuse had occurred. On the day we got together I felt confident and at peace about talking with them. It all came out over a cup of tea as we relaxed together. I began by telling them that I was writing this book. It ended with my dear Mum getting out of her seat and embracing me. We both wept and thanked the Lord and appealed to him together as we hugged. My Dad fully agreed and we hugged. Reconnection is the sweetest of times.

My mother's words and her response will always mean the world to me. My great concern all down the years was that my parents would not be embarrassed in front of their friends by all that had happened. This is one reason why I had suppressed things and kept it secret and why I was concerned for them now. My Mum said two things: 'Why shouldn't it be us?' and 'It has a happy ending'. How right she is. We are living in an unprecedented time when the sexual abuse of children is being shouted from the rooftops. She is right. Why shouldn't our family stand alongside all the other families who are prepared to suffer again. So that by exposing this evil we might stop others from experiencing the same trauma. The intention is not revenge but the restoring of lives.

Realistically, as long as evil exists, the sexual exploitation of the innocent will exist. Yes, Mum, let's put ourselves out there. Let us make people aware of the living nightmare perpetrators give their victims. Let us believe and pray that by the courageous stand of survivors some of the potential victims might not be targeted and never abused. That is our prayer. But also, that survivors might eventually become thrivers. Another step forward was attending the Independent Inquiry into Child Sexual Abuse, and when I travelled back to the cathedral to meet up with the new Dean and a Cannon it was a significant reconnection.

The happy ending? Sort of! The happy ending is that as a family we are closer than ever. Our relationships have never been bad, but just strained and at times distant. We are now open and have a depth in our relationships. I am happy that Sue is beginning to become free of the tyranny of my emotions. I am glad that I am less affected by them and that tsunamis are far less intense. There are some days when I see that I still have a long way to go and I do not yet have a happy ending. As Christians, we understand that we are not free from suffering yet and certainly not perfect! Suffering comes in many different forms and certain kinds of suffering are in service to Christ.[11] So we appreciate that the suffering we bear with Jesus releases the sweet aroma of Jesus.[12] That includes suffering to walk in the light with one another. Jesus is seen and known through it all.

Reconnection, though painful, is the sweetest of times. I am losing one world and gaining a much, much better one.

Section 3
Forgiven: The new identity in the aftermath

'I will give you the treasures of darkness, riches stored in secret places, so that you may know that I am the Lord, the God of Israel, who summons you by name.'

Isaiah 45:3

'Although I barely ever feel like a grown up … I realise that finally I'm "that chick", that woman, that I wanted to grow up to be.'

Rachel Lloyd, a survivor-thriver[I]

 To forgive or not to forgive?

> 'Nothing causes us to so nearly resemble God as the forgiveness of injuries.'
>
> John Chrysostom, a fourth century church leader[1]

Everyone we have met or worked with who has been abused says roughly the same thing: 'But I cannot forgive', 'I find it so hard to forgive' or, 'Do I have to forgive my abuser?' However, should we not be forgiving? Isn't that what God expects us to do?

For many years my understanding was that we forgive because God has forgiven us. I have preached, 'Forgiveness is For-Giving' 'Totally Forgiven, Totally Forgiving' and it is particularly the parable Jesus told about the unforgiving servant that gripped me and these final words: 'This is how my heavenly Father will treat each of you unless you forgive your brother from your heart'.[2]

One of the most gripping accounts of forgiveness that I have read was from Corrie Ten Boom after her terrible ordeals in the Ravensbruck concentration and extermination camp. She was the only survivor in her family, and after being released would speak to groups about the holocaust and forgiveness. After one talk a man approached her and said he had been a guard in the camp where she was, but he did not recognise her. She recognised him immediately and he explained he had since become a Christian and was asking for her forgiveness. Although frozen in horror she managed to put her hand out to shake his hand and say, 'I forgive you.' At that moment she experienced a flood of God's love come over her in a way she had not experienced before.

How do we reply to someone whose life has been torn apart by the evil actions of a callous, selfish individual and asks, 'Do I have to forgive my abuser?' What about those who have been treated so badly that they cannot forgive? I don't think that you are expected to forgive automatically, and it is not surprising that you cannot. God asks us to forgive like he has forgiven us.[3] So we need to know how he does that. He asks us to pray for our enemies and to love with His love. But we *are* expected to forgive under certain conditions.

If we look into the Scriptures and compare references, we find that God does not automatically forgive. Love is unconditional but forgiveness has conditions. Brian Edwards gives us a model of forgiveness that is derived from the way God forgives and it is most helpful.[4] It also helps us define and hold high some precious Bible words as vital actions:

REPENTANCE FORGIVENESS RECONCILIATION

The basis of this is that:

- God forgives us when we repent.
- God's forgiveness always results in reconciliation.
- God doesn't always forgive without repentance. But He does love unconditionally and shows mercy even if we haven't turned to Him.

This is how Edwards explains it:

'In society and the church, the big reason to forgive is too often to make the victim, and the rest of us, feel better. But does God forgive repentant sinners in order that *he* might feel better? The object of forgiveness is to make the *sinner* better, and he will never be better until he repents. On the other hand, compassion sheds tears. Healing for the Christian comes not from forgiving those who have sinned against you, but by trusting in the wisdom and love of God, humbly accepting his wise ways, and yearning with a compassion that leads to prayer, for the forgiveness by God of those who have wronged you.'[5]

Long ago I forgave the men who abused me because I thought it was the right thing to do. It was not a problem at the time because I knew how much God had forgiven me. My challenge is that I have found it difficult to forgive what I see as the needless offences of a few Christians. Jesus prayed for the Jews and Romans: 'Father, forgive them, for they do not know what they are doing'.[6] He prayed into the whole mission of His death. Often people offend us by the judgements they make or the actions they take whether in ignorance or not. My challenge is to look for every opportunity for repentance, forgiveness and reconciliation.

However, what if that person is unapproachable, dismissive or refuses to meet or has died?

Each day, I am to be like God and love unconditionally those who sin against me, to show mercy and not have bitterness gripping my heart. I am not under obligation to forgive them just to make me or others feel better, but I can pray with the Spirit of Jesus for them, that God should work repentance in their hearts bringing them to himself. I pray that my loving actions help, and so I release them into the Lord's supernatural work. At times, the best thing is to pray. I pray for blessing to be released in the heavily realms and for nothing but love in my heart towards them. I pray like Jesus: 'Father, forgive them, for they do not know what they are doing.' when there is repentance, I pray that I will forgive like God forgives. He chooses to ignore my sin, forget it and discard it so that I am permanently separated from it.[7] This includes agreeing with how God has forgiven me. I have found this to be as great a challenge as forgiving others.

My prayer for myself is that I will be up-to-date in my repenting, in my treatment of others and in knowing the abundant grace of God so that I will be able to truly forgive from my heart. I bear the responsibility to keep my heart right with God and leave him to bring his conviction to the hearts of others. The emphasis is more on me always being ready to ask for forgiveness. Living in repentance, by grace, giving unconditional love and treasuring reconciliation then has a deeper significance. The outstanding joy is that, like the woman who washed Jesus feet, I know God has forgiven me. The solid peace is that, through grace, I love and forgive those who have sinned against me. Whatever our view of forgiveness let us keep in mind that our closeness with God comes from a prayerful pursuit of forgiveness.

Chapter 15

'Friendly fire'

'Praise, my soul, the King of heaven,
To His feet thy tribute bring,
Ransomed, healed, restored, forgiven,
Who like thee His praise should sing?'

Henry F Lyte

Marilyn has a horrendous background, and after many years of support is now free from drug dependency. She has not worked on the streets for a couple of years now, since God made her His child. Though she is now free from her addictions and sexual exploitation, from time to time she is overcome by a tidal wave of feelings. She is now a grandmother, but like a child she leans on one of the team's shoulders during a Bible study: 'Why do I get so angry. I am at the end of myself and I don't want to be violent like I used to be. I know God has forgiven me. Is it wrong to feel like this? Are all my sins forgiven?'

Marilyn has been baptised and has attended church but there have been struggles and confrontations with other Christians. How can we deal with deep disappointments like these and make progress on our journey without becoming bitter or cynical? Surely the answer to these questions is our new identity as '*Ransomed, healed, restored, forgiven.*'

One of the dangers of serving in the armed forces and going into a war zone is being shot by your own troops. It is called 'friendly fire'. We are on a journey of restoration and part of it is coming to terms with 'friendly fire.' Something similar can happen in our own thoughts and feelings and also from what people say and do. Others can shoot us in the back but we can also shoot ourselves in the foot when we misinterpret what someone has said!

For many years I felt shut out by groups of Christians we were once close to. We tried to keep in touch but we seemed to be kept at arm's length.

There were harsh words or dismissive comments and times of being politely ignored. Perhaps we all give and take 'friendly fire'. It comes in different forms and most painfully from those we love the most. I can't but wonder if we are in this strange category of survivors from child abuse.

The most important thing is to know that we, in and through Jesus, are so completely forgiven that we are welcomed by our Father God with arms open wide. 'Ransomed, healed, restored, forgiven.' Knowing for sure that we are forgiven by an authoritative and unalterable decree from heaven, leads us into learning how to forgive others. We may never forget what has happened, but little by little we can learn to forgive.

Two characters who managed 'friendly fire' well

What a fascinating character Joseph is, with his technicolour dream-coat. His life was packed full of breakthroughs and setbacks, highs and lows, honours and undeserved punishments. It was pain, pain and more pain until one day there was reconciliation and the rescuing of thousands of lives.

If Joseph had a Facebook account (or a video diary) it might read something like this. 'I had an amazing dream that made me feel special and dad has made me an amazing cloak that makes me feel even more special.' 'Can't believe this. My brothers have thrown me into a pit and are about to sell me to slave traders!' 'Have a responsible job in charge of a busy and important house.' 'My master's wife has got me thrown into jail because I wouldn't give her what she wanted.' 'Been made president because God let me interpret the king's dreams.' 'Have a wonderful wife and two children.' 'Saving thousands from starvation.' 'Forgiven my brothers after they confessed.' 'Reconciled with all my whole family and we now live together here in Egypt.'

Joseph had a really great outlook that I do wish could have been in my thinking. Here it is: 'You were out to harm me, but God intended this for good.'[1] After a long journey, Joseph arrived at a place of significant personal healing. He caught hold of a higher vision than his own immediate experiences. This brought him in line with what God was doing so that his thinking was something like this: 'All of this, in every part, was God's plan to bring about his greater purpose and his ultimate good through me. Years and years of pain for me added up to years of gain for God's people relieved from famine and those beyond in future generations.' What is the Lord doing through you? None of it is easy. I have learnt to love and forgive but am relearning it. I'm also daring to see how I can reach others. Thank you Joseph.

Coping with 'friendly fire' leaves me utterly weak. It is embarrassing particularly when we are vulnerable. But it is right here that God looks at our complete weakness as the very condition that qualifies us to have his power poured in. Should I conclude then, that the Lord Himself wants to fill out this vacuum? The Lord has greater purposes than this, which we will come to a little later.

King David also experienced 'friendly fire'. He was severely rejected and hunted down by king Saul and later by his own son, Absalom. How did he cope with 'friendly fire' or a tsunami of emotions? He had dire and desperate times. No one can disagree with that. What he did was to depend on God and not on another human, nor even on himself.

HE WAS OPEN WITH GOD ABOUT HIS EMOTIONAL STATE TO THE POINT WHERE MOST OF US WOULD FIND HIM EMBARRASSING

The way he expresses himself is simply not 'British'! We cannot hide the fact that he was very expressive and let His God know in no uncertain terms exactly how he felt and what he was going through:

> 'My soul is in anguish. How long, O Lord, how long?'
>
> 'I am worn out from groaning, all night long I flood my bed with weeping and drench my couch with tears'.[2]
>
> 'My tears have been my food day and night.'
>
> 'Why are you so downcast, O my soul? Why so disturbed within me?'
>
> 'My soul is downcast within me …'
>
> 'My bones suffer mortal agony …'
>
> 'Why are you so downcast, O my soul? Why so disturbed within me?'[3]

David could hardly be more explicit about what he is experiencing emotionally. He had times that were extreme, for example his friendship with Jonathan ended tragically and abruptly.[4] He was on the run living in caves in the desert, hunted like an animal or a fugitive, when he was simply and honestly following the calling God had given him. The books of Samuel and Kings document these experiences well. At one point, he caused the death of eighty-five priests because they helped him; on another occasion, his family and the families of his men were captured by the enemy Amalekites. Then there was the time when he was brought down by the treachery of his own son, Absalom. In these experiences, he is embarrassingly honest about his emotional crisis. Some of these are self-inflicted, but most are unasked or 'friendly fire' and each of them controlled by God.

HE THREW HIMSELF INTO GOD'S ARMS (MOST OF THE TIME).

We don't know the timescale of some of these experiences. He could have been floundering for weeks or months when he was on the run from King Saul. He was in Gath, the enemy territory of King Achish, for sixteenth months.[5] Before this, he was on the run from Saul and hiding in the wilderness of Ziph. Some of his Psalms may well reflect these times. We cannot be certain about that, but we can be certain that he clung on to God with every finger and therefore couldn't cling to anything else. A baby rests back into the arms of a parent and at the same time wraps his little fingers around the parent's fingers. This is all that God wants us to do. Therefore, let us be careful to make these words our own words to our Lord God, our Father: 'Keep me safe, O God for in you I take refuge.' 'I have set the Lord always before me. Because He is at my right hand, I will not be shaken. Therefore my heart is glad and my tongue rejoices; my body also will rest secure'.[6] There are many other ways he says this to God.

HE ALLOWED GOD TO FULFIL HIS CRYING NEEDS.

This sounds so simple but of course it is not. He had years of experience in doing this. Only God can bind up the broken hearted. Only He has the power meet you in your weakness until you are not weak but strong. Let your own heart drink in David's experience with God so that it becomes your very heart with God:

> 'I waited patiently for the Lord; he turned to me and heard my cry. He lifted me out of the slimy pit ... He set my feet on a rock ... He put a new

> song in my mouth, a hymn of praise to my God. Blessed is the man who makes the Lord his trust.'
>
> 'Yet I am poor and needy; may the Lord think of me. You are my help and my deliverer; O my God, do not delay.'
>
> 'Satisfy us in the morning with your unfailing love, that we may sing for joy and be glad all our days.'[7]

In each time of his need the Lord provided, and he did not search out his own solution or satisfaction somewhere else.

HE CAME TO A PLACE OF ADORATION IN MAKING GOD AND NOT HIS SITUATION THE CENTRE OF HIS ATTENTION.

David's aim in writing Psalms is to inspire heart-worship in others as well as himself. I get the impression that He didn't intend to spill out everything just for the sake of it. But was leading his people into the presence of God from the stark realities of what they were experiencing so that they might be consumed with and by God:

> 'My heart is steadfast, O God; I will sing and make music with all my soul. Awake, harp and lyre! I will awaken the dawn. I will praise you, O Lord, among the nations; I will sing of you among the peoples. For great is your love, higher than the heavens; your faithfulness reaches to the skies. Be exalted, O God, above the heavens, and let your glory be over all the earth'.[8]

A new day was dawning. Time shut away with Jesus is time spent well. At college, I could sneak away to one of the prayer rooms and be alone with the Lord. King David, as the man after God's heart, needed to be in God's deep embrace. I had to learn that there were no shortcuts and I needed time alone with God. I spent a good chunk of a day praising my heavenly Father through the tears. How good, deeply good, it was to adore Almighty God and see him at the centre of it all. Thank God for praisesongs on YouTube!

Surely it is God's desire for us to be so utterly consumed with Him that we drink from His river of delight to be refreshed there, so that our thirst is quenched by Him: 'Taste and see that the Lord is good: blessed is the man who takes refuge in him'.[9] Then having tasted, we hide away in him and live satisfied in him and protected by him: 'With my mouth I will greatly extol the Lord; in the great throng I will praise him. For he stands at the right hand of the needy one, to save his life from those who condemn him.'[10]

I am usually open with God, but do not always throw myself into his arms. If I can do this and depend on him to fulfil my crying need I will have made the Lord the epicenter of my world and will worship Him heartily: 'I will extol the Lord with all my heart in the council of the upright and in the assembly.'[11]

What do we have as an alternative to this even when friends fail us? We can be pampering ourselves in one moment and beating ourselves up in the next. Be gentle and clear with yourself. Treat yourself as the Lord treats you. Allow yourself to be led back into God's presence. Even when you are consumed with other loves. Even when you cannot fathom the outcome or what the future holds. Even when you don't feel like it or are in tears. Even when you feel isolated, misunderstood, alone. Go to God. This is what the prodigal son did (repenting) and look at the welcome he had and the new life he discovered![12]

Chapter 16

Hope—out of no hope

'The Bible has a great deal to say about suffering and most of it is encouraging.'

A W Tozer.

Sue and I met after a church service when back from college. I was rather lonely and had asked the Lord for a wife. Then, when I saw her from the back of the church, I prayed that He would introduce me to this lovely young lady. My prayer was answered and we were married just over a year later.

We were not aware at the time that PTSD interrupted the romantic phases in our relationship. It seemed to us that we had challenges like any other married couple. Many years later, when we were back at college for a different purpose, Sue and I discovered that we are at opposite ends of the personality spectrum and as such, so it was said, completely unsuited to one another. Add that into the mix of ME (chronic fatigue syndrome) and the childhood trauma, it really is a miracle that Sue and I are together.

Do you remember the woman in Luke 7:36–50 who anointed Jesus with her perfume? She poured out all her perfume on Jesus so extravagantly because he had released her from her scarred past. Her breakthrough was not a tiny light but a blinding revelation. Everything in her past that contaminated her and clogged her up was washed clear away giving her a new capacity for love. Another miracle of hope from Jesus. Bible hope is much bigger than any other because it involves being held by someone and something bigger than ourselves. This is what we badly needed in our marriage.

Our past had been washed away and the Lord was unclogging us. Was there something in our marriage that we could do to move on, even with just small steps? My role as husband is to behave as Christ does, with unconditional, non-condemning love. Expressing that extravagantly in a way Sue could receive was the challenge. The adventure of a new beginning was something that I found exciting; something that had the potential of stirring up the embers. It was a new dawn of a new day which I prayed might be refreshing for us both, but particularly for Sue. As always this happened very slowly and with faltering, painful but significant steps. I will leave Sue to write about this in the next chapter, which is hers.

Our root mission statement is in a Scripture that Sue was looking at again. She noted how much of Jesus' work was directed at those who are grieving. His mission statement was taken from Isaiah 61:

> 'He has sent me to bind up the *broken-hearted* ... to comfort all who *mourn*, and provide for those who *grieve* in Zion—to bestow on them a crown of beauty instead of *ashes*, the oil of gladness instead of *mourning*, and a garment of praise instead of a spirit of *despair*'.[1]

More than a half of Jesus' own mission was towards those who are broken. But there is more to notice. The Lord reconstructs and renovates these lives so that they in turn are made able to 'rebuild' and 'renew' others.[2] The Lord also intends to do something else for these demolished then reconstructed people. He intends to take away their shame and give them a double portion so that they rejoice instead. This is what verse 7 says:

> 'Instead of their shame my people will receive a double portion, and instead of disgrace they will rejoice in their inheritance; and so they will inherit a double portion in their land, and everlasting joy will be theirs.'

How refreshing and positively inspiring it is to see the contrast the Lord makes: shame and disgrace versus a double portion of joy. Here is this assurance he gives, that they will settle or come home to 'their land'. This was a direct prophecy for Israel then. The Messiah, as anointed preacher, will bring his transformed people into a renewed world. Thank you, Lord. This is now our mission and it is our testimony. I should make it my responsibility to remind the Lord of his great promises here. He alone can do this, and he has said that he will.

Jesus takes this up in His first sermon: 'Blessed are those who mourn, for they shall be comforted'.[3] The real issue for the woman with the perfume is not what she gave to Jesus, but what he had already given to her. It was not what she was doing for him, but what he had done for her. The deep and extravagant thankfulness she exuberantly expressed was for a refreshing and transforming sense of forgiveness that she had already been given. A death is not often good news, but her past was now dead and buried and this was ecstatic news. It is this revelation which made her mourn with thankfulness. God turns our sin life into a thoroughly forgiven life so that Jesus can say, 'Blessed (happy) are those who mourn.'

I could take you to a church this Sunday where you would be welcomed on the door with such a rich, full and pure love that you will want to go back the following week. We could drive from there to the other side of town and visit another dear saint whose spirit is so encouragingly sweet, with the joy and gentleness of Jesus, that you wish you could bottle it to be poured out and sweeten others who have the opposite spirit.

My privilege is in knowing many sweet-spirited people who share this in common: They have all suffered abuse or a trauma, but have been blessed by God so that their spirit has been renewed. Now there is a distinct spiritual perfume on them; a beauty that they are unaware of that makes them beautiful people. It is a 'crown of beauty instead of ashes.' The Lord has done this. In our suffering, in the unjust evils we face and the cruelty, God makes us aware of His great blessings and we become a blessing to others. Under his blessing we are given his deep, deep comfort.

The woman with the perfume is understood to have been a prostitute—and she was washing the feet of Jesus with her own tears; her 'heart water' says Luther. She has a brand new hope of being with Jesus for ever because everything she has done is now taken away by Jesus. All that has been done to her has been taken by Jesus. Like her, we who are brokenhearted, who mourn, who grieve or despair and receive from Jesus, have the same deep hope and profound blessing. God keeps his promises. He exchanges our shame for his double portion of grace; our disgrace for rejoicing in his inheritance. Our new identity is packed full of hope.

A word from Sue

This chapter tells my story as a companion to my husband. The survivor's journey is perplexing and I trust my account will give insight and a strategy of hope.

The beginning of our journey together

'I was abused when I was at boarding school', Rob said, as we sat at the bus stop talking on a more intimate level. 'Oh,' I replied, thinking along the lines of many horrible beatings. We were dating and our relationship was deepening. My admission of pre-Christian, teenage, behaviour was to give him opportunity to back out now, well before there was a thought of marriage. I mused naively that his disclosure did not equal the gravity of mine.

Rob is an extrovert, well liked, an entertainer, passionate, creative, an optimist, a gifted teacher. When I first met him, he presented to me as confident, capable, expert in everything—a real find! His bold character was, and still is, the perfect match for my introverted, quiet steadiness. And so, we were married in 1977.

What marriage does not have its problems? The problems are manageable when you also enjoy companionship as we did. We were good friends with much in common, but from the beginning I felt a failure as a wife, because Robert seemed to live in a state of dissatisfaction and frustration with our relationship.

Training for ministry and Myalgic Encephalomyelitis (ME)

Rob was a Teacher of Art and then, after a few years of marriage, he trained as a pastor. Those years of biblical training in the local church rooted us firmly into God's word. Generally, we benefited from the clear interpretation and application of Scripture into every part of our life. I was given fabulous tools for Bible understanding, and it helped me develop a close walk with God and smoothed the way for peace in our relationship.

His role as Assistant Pastor and simultaneous Principal of the church-based Christian School was totally absorbing and meant a sixty plus hour week for Rob. Not listening to warning signs, and enjoying the adrenaline of success, gave opportunity for the ME virus to take hold.

The following few years proved very difficult as the ME symptoms were misunderstood as malingering. This is a catalyst for depression and anxiety for anyone, but combined with the underlying symptoms of PTSD and fears of failure, threatening his good standing in the community, made it devastating. Suddenly the pressure was on our marriage as well. I felt shut out from him, yet he yearned for more of me and my time. And so began the perplexing emotions: anger and frustration and an emotional push and pull.

The Middle Years: growing grumblings and another house move

We moved to the West Midlands in 1988 for Rob to take up the pastorate of a small church. He managed to fulfil his responsibilities whilst trying to stabilise the ME. God blessed the work in the church, and our congregation were a source of great joy during our years there.

After the birth of our fifth child, however, I suffered Post Natal Depression. At the same time, Rob was managing some pastoral challenges within the church. Meanwhile unpleasant 'scenario's' repeatedly played out within our marriage that made me feel inadequate. And, to make matters worse, Rob was battling with a relapse of ME. Because of all this we decided that Rob should come out of church ministry. We moved back to our old house at Christmas 1994 and he returned to teaching.

Far from easing the pressure, being out of the ministry caused Rob grief. He was not in a good place. The 'scenarios' continued, hallmarked by emotional intensity and high drama. Long bewildering late-night inquisitions would leave me emotionally exhausted, sapped dry.

Here is an example of our drama:

Life is ticking by nicely and we are enjoying mutual companionship. I notice he has become anxious, quiet and withdrawn. I brace myself. He cannot settle and needs to talk. He accuses: I have neglected him significantly and we should book regular slots in our diary so it doesn't happen again. I have misunderstood him, been too tired, too busy, not taken hints, have failed to make him feel special. In my mind, we are enjoying good connection on every level. He goes on to explain further, but I do not understand him at all. Over the following hours, sometimes days, my resolve to remain positive weakens and I am overwhelmed. My natural reaction to rationalise just fuels his anguish. I am at fault and my every move is evidence to confirm his fears. My connection and companionship with him is dwindling as is my confidence. In total innocent frustration, he says he loves me and holds nothing against me.

God begins to change me first!

Struggling with responsibility of the home, children, Rob, and adding self-preservation and sinful escapes to the mix, I was in a spiral of despair. It was in this pressure pot that I finally ran dry of my own resources. God had gained my full attention. I turned back to Him and began to read my Bible differently, meticulously putting into practice what I learned, depending on God for my very breath. If I couldn't do anything else, I decided I would be the best Christian ever! I had nothing to lose.

My decision began a journey with God that was absolutely transforming. I discovered that, in abandoning my natural instinct for self-preservation, and leaning wholly on God, His principles really did work. It wasn't difficult. As I read my Bible it was just one small thing at a time, one principle put into practice a day at a time. The way I began to think and live sprung from what I read. Here are some notes of the process that unfolded over the next few years:

- Thankfulness.[1] I felt prompted purposefully to list anything I could think of that was good. And I thanked God for each. After the children had left for school I took a few minutes each day. It was a discipline to begin with but the list began to flow as I worked on it regularly. I started to feel lighter and enjoy my daily responsibilities.
- Love doesn't fail.[2] I was keeping a journal, and one day as I turned to the next page, there was a print of Claude Monet's painting of the sun breaking through fog over the Houses of Parliament with the River Thames in the foreground. What hope stirred in me that morning. It reminded me of God's powerful love. A love that pierces sin. A love that is kind and unconditional. Can I love like that? I wanted to, and the idea hung there as I sat before God. I began to

overlook my husband's short comings and thank God for him. Most importantly of all I began to pray for God's blessing to be upon him in every way. The Lord's Prayer became a template and I found liberty before God to pray deep prayers over every part of Rob's life.

- Fill your heart with good things. You are what you think.[3] Where were my thoughts day by day? On what was I feeding my mind? I began to store up a bank of good things; seeking out good worship music, helpful books and making the most of positive company. Look after your heart (do it good!).[4]
- Oh! to be free of the sin that so easily entangles and to run the race.[5] A sin that had become a snare to me was incredibly difficult to get free of. In the end, it was through confession to a close and wise friend who stood by me in prayer that God finally broke the bondage.[6]
- Where was my treasure?[7] What motivated me each day, because that is where my heart would be. My life needed re-orientating and God was becoming my all in all.
- God is no killjoy.[8] He has come to give me life, not take it. During this period, we pursued a counsel session at a local church and booked a 'Freedom In Christ' day. This proved to be pivotal for me. The day itself was fairly uneventful, but it provided an opportunity for a prayerful, spiritual overhaul. One thing I was convicted of was the thought that I did not trust God to have my best interests at heart. Was He not just a taskmaster with a clipboard? Once my error was revealed, I was so sorry before God. I have since tried and tested and learned that nothing else comes close to the joy and life He gives.
- I am *very* precious to God. I am the apple of His eye.[9] Wonder of wonders, God really loves *me*!
- God has heard my cry. He will send from heaven and save me.[10] He did not afflict willingly nor will he reject for ever.[11] Accept that the words in the Bible are for me. Here is God's heart for us. He is not arbitrary in His dealing, but very specific. If we are suffering—bring it on—it is for our growth! This is the right attitude referred to in Hebrews 12:11ff.
- Do not fall short of God's grace.[12] This is the antidote to bitterness.

What is the point of trying to work out why we are experiencing tough times? I found that by simply accepting my circumstances as 'allowed' by my loving Father in Heaven I could count on Him for strength and grace to embrace every hurdle with enthusiasm, patience and hopefulness. Or repent when clearly convicted by God.

- God has heard and drawn near, redeemed my life and works all things together for good.[13]
- Do not refuse Him who is asking.[14] Scary but the joy of seeing God come through is exhilarating, as in the following two points.
- As I walk the harrowing path between accusing lions,[15] God keeps me. He keeps me breathing His breath, depending on His word, He alone is my lifeline. There were times when I felt accused, condemned and guilty. I had to learn to look to God who alone tests our hearts and motives. Often, it turned out, God did not accuse me. How liberating to be found clothed in God-given righteousness. I began to maintain a clear conscience before God.[16]
- Wait for God.[17] Do not run for cover. Your help *must* come from God.[18] My natural reaction to fear, was to retreat and run. This is absolutely not what God wanted of me. In the heat and crisis of the moment God wanted me to commit my way to him and depend on Him for the outcome.[19]
- Do not lean on your own understanding nor be wise in your own eyes (Proverbs 3:4,5). What wise counsel. This advice has stood me in good stead when so many times the situation I was facing was illogical and irrational.
- Because I am precious to God, He is on my case.[20] I am not helpless.
- This is God's love for me—chosen while still filthy.[21]
- Forgiveness is substitutional. Jesus gives us His righteousness while He takes our sin.[22] So too we forgive and release our debtor while freely and willingly bearing the consequences of the injustice against us.
- The sweetness of God's word strengthened and carried me.[23]
- Create an appetite for God.[24] I had tasted how good God is and I didn't want to become complacent. Therefore, I would deliberately come into the presence of God mentally replacing contentment with a desire for more of God. Or if the desire just wasn't there at all, then asking God to change my heart.

- Getting active and busy, looking out for other people in the community, was a deliberate attitude I took on to break out of self-absorption. It grew into a fruitful time as I discovered many other hurting people whose needs I could think about meeting.[25]

Amazing things began to happen

As I clung to Jesus I was seeing our circumstances so much more clearly, and there was a softening between us. I was also discovering my own significance in God's eyes.

I was observing aspects to Rob that I had been blind to before; at the same time God was also reminding me that He had called Rob to the pastorate. He did it fully knowing all. It was no mistake. And God was using him in the building of His kingdom. I was being reminded to respect Rob in his role as my husband and head of our home; respect the mantle of leadership God has placed upon him whilst recognising his humanity. He was gifted and called—and human!

Opportunity to pray fell from heaven! Rob was working away from home Monday to Friday and I had a regular free day once a week as all the children were either at college, school or preschool and I was freer in the evenings and at night. Confidence and certainty that prayer was the only way forward became a conviction and a passion. The Lord's prayer and other writers were my inspiration.[26] Many, scriptures became my platform. I had a strong sense that the hours of fasting, praying and wrestling with God were significant. Especially when, at the pinnacle of those weeks, I had a black and horrifying experience in the middle of one night. Suffice it to say that vocalising the name of Jesus alone, brought about an immediate sense of safety. The amazement of that night has remained with me as I felt that something awesome had occurred though I was not sure what.

However, the negative and destructive 'scenarios' *still* repeated periodically. This I could not understand, given my utter surrender to God and belief in His good purpose. We did not appreciate the root of Rob's anxieties and frustrations, the pain of rejection he experienced so regularly from me, nor the agony of emotion that tormented him. All were symptoms of childhood abuse, but I did not know this at the time.

Revelation arrives!

Our own strange journey of nearly going to Sierra Leone in January 2013 to work as missionaries was part of God's restorative plan. Through this life change, a period of about two years, I began to research modern day slavery and the plight of vulnerable women. I came across two books: *The White Umbrella* by Mary Frances Bowley and *Trauma and Recovery* by Judith Herman. These began to unpack an identification with, and an understanding of, PTSD.

There, on many pages of Judith Herman's book, I recognised Rob and myself. Herman was describing our situation. Words and phrases and explanations began to put behaviour, reactions and comments into a context. Although I did not understand how Rob could be threatened by abandonment or rejection within our relationship.

'The need for control is a desperate attempt to defend against abandonment.'[27] I began to learn that an innocently made comment by me or an action or situation, could trigger rejection, torment and terror in Rob, and the negatives spiral disproportionately. It is known as Rejection and Abandonment.

We needed support to 'navigate' us through this new world of understanding. Support came in the form of prayer partners, spiritual and practical counsellors, accountability and therefore connection to the community around us. I learned that I was responsible for defining boundaries for my own safety and growth.

> 'Personal boundaries are the physical, emotional and mental limits we establish to protect ourselves from being manipulated, used, or violated by others. They allow us to separate who we are, and what we think and feel, from the thoughts and feelings of others.'[28]

The following quote has helped me identify *my* standards of acceptable behaviour as I relate to others. What makes me uncomfortable? What do I consider appropriate that keeps my relationship with others safe? Being boundary-aware helps me stay connected without the need to withdraw.

> 'Sometimes unconditional love can be confused with accepting unconditional behaviour with no boundaries. This never works, so barriers are erected to protect us and confuse our message. Our unconditional values get diluted and conditional love is trapped in boundaries and barriers ... How is unconditional love communicated through me? Do I have boundaries or barriers? I realise this is a massive

> subject. Some will find peace in boundaries while others could scramble for barriers. What does unconditional love look like for me? How do we navigate towards Isaiah 53 and Philippines 2?'[29]

Telling the Story—walking in the light

I had begun to talk to Rob about what I was seeing in the two books. He was so interested that he too began reading. Within a couple of months, we were acknowledging that the legacy of child abuse had been interfering with our intimacy. And we were beginning to talk about looking for professional counsel.

Breaking the silence and beginning to talk about the years of hidden pain has been unspeakably consoling. I began by talking with a parent and then a sibling. I asked for prayer from a trusted sister in Christ. The process I went through of humility and transparency with wise and trusted friends was blessed by God. They affirmed me and supported me out of confusion, guilt and condemnation. Light, clarity, hope and therefore, healing ensued. How freeing and rewarding is a strong connection to the wider community.

At last we had words to describe the problem, but *still* the scenarios were periodically re-occurring and every time they happened I was floored.

And so the restorative process continued …

It was a fight to keep focused on the need for togetherness and not to let the apparent catastrophes rob me of the knowledge that 'all things work together for good', and, 'Walk by faith and not by sight'.[30] I must believe God just like Abraham did: how will God work?,[31] and be confident in God's willingness to answer prayer—in His way. Oh! what dark days and how we floundered! But God loves marriage and wants it to succeed, to reflect Christ and the Church.[32]

About the spiritual battle

Jesus said that some things cannot change without prayer and fasting.[33] Although I cannot claim to have done much fasting, it was when I set my heart to both fasting and prayer that the two biggest breakthroughs happened.

We have an *enemy that twists the truth*. He is out to steal, kill and destroy.[34] The work of the enemy is an evil business. He is ruthless and cruel. Once he has blighted a young life with a trauma, he has won multiple opportunities to gain a foothold and create havoc with relationships even to bring a premature end to a life!

Recognise the lie that says it is your fault, you are to blame. Is your own situation unclear as to what has gone wrong? Are you in a miry pit? Have you been led to believe you are 'not enough'. The lie confuses the reality of your own real shortfalls with feelings of condemnation and worthlessness. Through guilt it paralyses. It robs of confidence and isolates. It makes you feel that no one can understand and there is none to whom you can turn for help. Revelation 12:10 tells us that Satan is the accuser of the brethren, but the name of Jesus is powerful to overcome. His name alone, together with the prayers of the saints, cut through deception and condemnation. 'Do not be overcome by evil but overcome evil with good'.[35]

Learn to dress daily in *the armour of God* that you may be able to stand against the schemes of the enemy. The victim mentality says, I cannot say 'No. I cannot bear the painful, hostile consequences of saying no to control and manipulation.' But God says, 'be strong and courageous'. God says, 'be strong in the Lord ... put on the whole armour of God, that you may be able to stand against the schemes of the devil.'[36] Sometimes it is appropriate to be silent before your accusers. Jesus is our example. At other times it is entirely right to speak out against opposition.[37]

Jesus is able. *The name of Jesus is powerful.* He is sufficient. God knows when we are ready for the next stage of battle and 'occupation of the new land'. God says, 'I will not give your enemies into your hand all in one go, because the land will be too great for you to manage. The Lord our God will drive out your enemies little by little' (my paraphrase). 'The battle is the lord's. Stand firm.[38]

If you have any doubts about the authenticity of Scripture why not settle it in your heart today? Once and for all to accept every dot and tittle as sovereignly preserved for our direction and benefit. See how this changes your growth in faith! Jesus is our example to follow. So, emulate Him. Pray like Him. You can be sure that if you pray like Jesus it will be wonderfully pleasing to your Father in Heaven.

A breakthrough

The words 'rejection' and 'wrong expectation' were coming to me time and again. Are these at the heart of Rob's discomfort and disquiet? We were working hard to progress our relationship yet were having many more frequent conflicts. Finally, I voiced my belief that he had an unresolved issue with rejection, and added that I suspected he also carried wrong expectations of me. Rob's response frightened me as he felt there was absolutely no way forward any more. This, after a thirty-eight-year struggle to do and maintain God's perfect plan for marriage—till death us do part, for better or worse. Including numerous counsellors, several attempts at seeking wisdom from fellow pastors, and praying of course. For Rob, the option for us to remain under the same roof was unsustainable with the dynamics as they were. Sadly, I resignedly began to outline the most amicable first steps towards marital separation.

Rejection and Wrong Expectation Acknowledged

It is interesting what happens when you get to rock bottom. The following morning, Rob emerged from a sleepless night acknowledging how rejection works in his psyche. More than this, he had wrestled through with a method of countering it, complete with accountability written in. This is *his* solution to *his* problem. *He* hatched it with God in the night watches, *he* will take it into his daily life and involve a trusted friend. Amazing!

Something more happened in Rob a few weeks later after visiting a friend. I am clueless as to what happened, but as a result, I no longer felt the hold of unreasonable expectation. I believe he had taken control of another powerful bastion removing it from hurting our marriage.

Growing away from co-dependancy

One day, Rob described to me a moment of turbulent feelings as a 'merry-go-round' of emotions. My world was rocking again as I felt the potential of another scenario unfolding. I was tempted to despair but God opened my eyes: Can I do my part in giving Rob space to allow a healthy distance between us, so that he can remain the amazing, creative and emotionally sensitive person he is? Can I value him and rejoice in our distinct differences? In other words, can I activate a safe 'boundary' of levelheadedness to protect my heart and leave the responsibility of managing his roller-coaster of negative emotions entirely to him? As I pondered, yes. I felt safe—and optimistic. Is it possible now, to grow towards carefree confidence in 'us', reaping the years of investment into our shared life together? Suddenly there is freedom—and Hope.

Reconnection

Rob has earlier written of 'reconnection'. Rob and I have discovered that sharing the Lord's Supper together makes for an opportunity to check our spirits in a relationally horizontal way that does not necessarily happen in our alone times with God. It triggers transparency, unity and true fellowship.

I am proud of my dear husband. Throughout, he has doggedly held on to faith in God in spite of the terror and anguish within. He has bravely faced the darkest and deepest secret of his abuse that kept him from transparent and intimate relationships. Now everything is in the light, the darkness of the past can no longer hurt him. He has been reconnecting a new him, the real him, with peers and colleagues.

Rob truly is a changed man. It is now clear that God has done a thorough healing work in him overcoming the fallout from the hideous things that should never have occurred in his childhood. Whilst he continues to re-establish himself I too am learning to reconnect with him emotionally and discover anew my role as his wife and helpmeet.

> Trust in the Lord with all your heart,
> and do not lean on your own understanding.
> In all your ways acknowledge him,
> and he will make straight your paths.
> Be not wise in your own eyes;
> fear the Lord, and turn away from evil.
> It will be healing to your flesh
> and refreshment to your bones.
>
> Proverbs 3:5–8

Conclusion

When children are exposed to trauma, their undeveloped emotions are stunted. The abused child quickly learns how to blend seamlessly into the world around them whilst blocking out the unmanageable. The brain is an amazing mechanism that can disassociate from reality, thereby allowing the owner to fit into his social world. The coping strategies can become complex. It is not surprising then that restoration in adulthood is usually slow and complex.

Chapter 17

I am thoroughly blessed by observing God's tender, loving way that uses time and procedure to achieve true freedom and liberation. It is exampled in His detailed, patient, long suffering attendance to the children of Israel as He brought them out of their four-hundred-year period of slavery under Egyptian tyranny, establishing first their sense of identity, their self-governance, and their growing understanding, trust and obedience to God and leading them through a forty-year period in the wilderness to the time when they will be strong to confront Jericho with its impenetrable walls. Thereafter to *slowly* and *steadily* take sustainable occupation of the bountiful 'Promised Land.' I find Deuteronomy 7:21–22 fascinating in this context. God knows not to give such vast freedoms too soon, and kindly explains that 'enemies will be cleared little by little … lest wild beasts grow too numerous for you'.

Glorious transformation is realised by the commitment of one little step at a time and I get the strong feeling that God is more than OK with the inevitable stumbling and circling. He loves us! Note Israel's many relapses and rebukes that are characteristic of the journey made by people today seeking restoration.

I hope the principle comes through clearly, that God uses circumstances for the good of all. God involves me, because, in the process I am cornered, exposed and offered opportunity to grow too! By faith, I can say, I recognise this journey has been important for me and I need never again feel a victim.

As we live out the practicalities of walking free from exploitation I find that I have not been an overt part of the solution. Neither of us recognised what was going on. It was certainly never my job to fix Rob! Transformation is a slow process. It is God's process. Beware of of the temptation to fix people!

'A threefold cord is not easily broken'.[39] Thank God that He runs through and around our relationship. It has held together against all the odds. Thanks be to God.

My heartfelt thanks go to Dave and Di, Jen, Nic, Cat, Lucie, Heather, Elizabeth, Sonya, Ruth, Both Mum's and Dad's.

A Healing Strategy for the Soul Wounds of Rejection and Abandonment

'Change takes place not merely when certain changes occur, but only when there has been a change. The change of an activity is not the same as the change of a person. The former may involve actions sporadically or temporary sustained by certain conditions; the latter involves a pattern of development as part of the fabric of a person's life that brings about those actions in spite of the conditions.'

J E Adams[I]

For years I tried to give up smoking. Since early teens, I had enjoyed nicotine in various forms but now I was going to a church where it seemed that I was the only one who did! I desperately wanted to change this habit but found again and again I didn't have enough will power to do it. Cutting down wasn't a problem. But stopping didn't last for long. It took three or four years to stop completely, and some strange experiences along the way.

I gave my roll-up packs to my father-in-law and bought a couple of pipes. That made me feel better for a while. When I tried to quit smoking pipes I couldn't, even though it made the washing smell. After plumbing in a new central heating system and laying back the wooden floor, one of my pipes disappeared; then my favourite pipe was crushed under the wheel of our car. I had left it on the ground at a petrol station while filling up with fuel. I then graduated to cigars. An ash tray was kept in the top draw of the filing cabinet just in case one the elders of the church paid us a visit!

The motivation for all this was partly that I wanted to be like the non-smokers around me. But a more powerful thought gripped me. Wasn't I a sacred place where God, the Holy Spirit had set up home?[2] This combined with an answer to prayer, and lasting change arrived at last!

Change for someone suffering from a childhood trauma is not merely a change of a habit but a change in living and it begins with changes in thinking. Eventually on my journey of restoration what I wanted to change the most was the injury I was causing Sue. I was desperate to stop discouraging, hurting and offending her with my negative feelings and harsh words. After months of counselling we both began to see my problem with rejection and abandonment was the main issue. This erupted in sporadic but relentless negative episodes. The tsunamis might have lessened in intensity but the minor tremors were still destructive. Like my experience with quitting smoking I needed one final breakthrough.

Throughout this book, I have mentioned that there are many approaches available that help restore the life of a victim of abuse. Psychologists, psychotherapists, prayer for inner healing and biblical counselling, have all helped us in varying degrees. God does work in various ways and Jesus approached people's needs in a variety of ways. When it comes to lasting change I have found that for it to be effective it needs, as Jay Adams wrote,'to involve a pattern of development as part of the fabric of a person's life that brings about those actions in spite of the conditions.'

Change in my activities is one thing; change in me as a person is another. I cannot change my past; it is gone. Unless you give me a time machine, I cannot go back and make alterations. But step-by-step changes in me will change the influence my past has on me. I cannot change my past by self-punishment nor my future by worrying. Both are a waste of emotional energy. I know this and yet I can still fret. What I need to do is embrace change now in the present and that will affect the future. It was changes in thought-habits that would determine changes in feelings and actions

Over a period of four years, since recognising the effects of child abuse, I still hit times where I felt abandoned, unwanted and surplus to requirements. We could see these growing less and less but a reoccurrence caused us both serious problems particularly when it was combined with a bout of ME. It came to a point where we just could not go on in this way and, as Sue has mentioned in the previous chapter, we even talked about divorce as an option. That night I went to my bed totally despondent and cried again to Jesus for His intervention. Sue and I were really good friends. I thought we had tried everything but it had come to this.

Early the next morning, I woke up with an idea that gave me hope in our hopelessness. If there is a downward spiral into abandonment and rejection then there has to be an upward one. I am all too familiar with slipping down into a dark pit of despair. The Lord has promised that we have Jesus as our bed rock.[3] There has to be a ladder somewhere that He can give me to climb out of this. I grabbed a piece of file paper and started to draw and write. This is what I came up with. (see Chart 3)

By the grace of God, I had found the way out of the long-trodden maze. Identification with the stages of negativity on the left side was easy enough. What was needed were steps and thought-patterns that would break me out of this slide of isolation and take me back into connectedness. Sue helped me to see that I could easily misinterpret what she said. It was also my natural response to have a negative as my first thought (auto-negative). If, for example, Sue had a busy diary I would think that she preferred to spend time with other people. Can't really blame her of course (!), but that was not what she was thinking.

It did not take long to develop a habit of grabbing a positive thought. The negative and positive could then stand side by side and I chose which thought I would accept. We have also developed a habit of exchanging positive things about our day over our evening meal. This began to train the auto-negative to be auto-positive. Changes in thought-habits determine changes in feelings and actions.

Now, that is on a good day! However, when I am tired or ill or feeling vulnerable, it is easy to slide down the left side of negative responses. It will then take more effort to jump away into the positive. But having tasted the difference that the upward spiral brings to relationships and to general well-being, the effort is charged with motivation. At any point, I can swing across to the other side and start rising out of the mess. When I have slipped down into a minus three, the feelings are vile, so it takes a more aggressive 'thought jump' to stand on the positive. If I am more seriously down in a minus four then I need to humbly ask for help from a trusted friend. What makes this work is having friends in place and having healthy alternatives ready to hand.

The powerful life-transplant described for us in Romans 6 establishes a

CHART 3

Downward or upward spiral

-1 A negative statement or experience
The 'NO' factor
FEELINGS OF REJECTION

-2 A false interpretation
THOUGHTS OF REJECTION

-3 Rapid negative thinking
AVALANCHE OF REJECTION

-4 Hopeless isolation—anger, bitterness, resentment
CONSOLIDATION OF REJECTION

-5 Attempts to deaden pain
ALTERNATIVE GRABBING

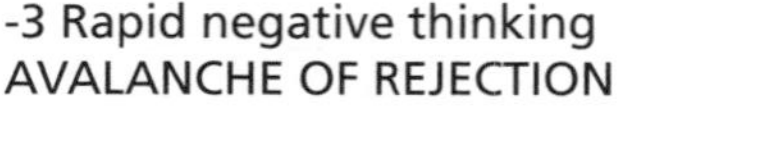

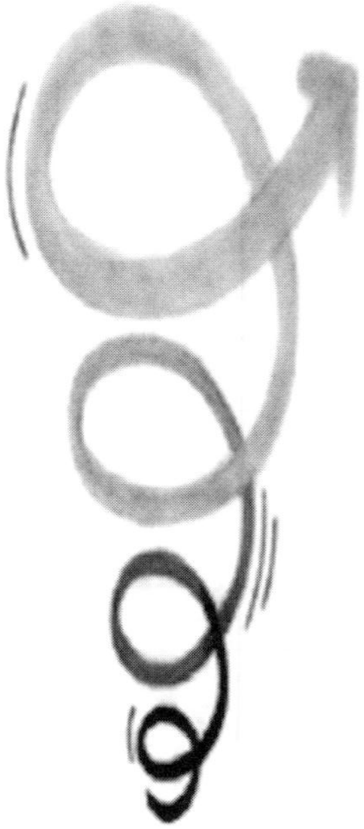

SEPARATION
momentarily, as a regular pattern or as a permanent condition

TOGETHERNESS/INTIMACY

+1 A positive statement or experience
The 'YES' factor
FEELINGS THAT ARE POSITIVE

+2 The true interpretation
THOUGHTS THAT ARE TRUE

+3 The arrest and rejection of negative thinking to stand on positive thoughts
AGGRESSIVE RESISTANCE

+4 Phone a friend—make a hopeful connection
CONSOLATION OF A COMPANION

+5 Healthy alternatives
Music, a film, a walk, art or photography
ALTERNATIVES THAT ARE HEALTHY

radically different way of thinking. Joining Jesus in His death means we are dead to sin and alive in Christ through His resurrection.[4] Because of this we are no longer slaves to sin but our new master is grace and righteousness.[5] This life-transplant is described as living by the Spirit in Galatians 5:16–26 which transforms our desires, attitudes and actions. This entirely different way of living requires us to 'put off, put on' desires and actions.[6] By 'putting off the old self' we can be 'made new in the attitudes of (our) minds'.[7] This is an entirely new way to think and live, most effectively developed by meditating in God's word. The powerful life-transplant enables us to be 'transformed by the renewing of (our) minds' which for most of us is a lifetime journey one day at a time.[8]

Restoration is inside out and outside in. Both my working on changes and the inner work of God have to be present. Life in the Spirit, which is the default for us as new creations, means a mind controlled by the Spirit.[9] There were initial changes in my actions but it has become changes in my thoughts, attitudes and motivations which have led to the greatest changes in me. Thankfully over it all is an ongoing healing of wounds by the One who came to 'bind up the brokenhearted'. God's work and my collaboration have led to a greater togetherness in our marriage. But I think it fair to say that for both of us it has often been a really rough road.

Chapter 19

A brand new beginning

'If anyone is in Christ, he is a new creation. The old has passed away, behold, the new has come.'

2 Corinthians 5:17

Jonathan turned up on our doorstep on a weekly basis, sometimes in the middle of the night. He was usually agitated or angry and, on one occasion, violent. Then there were the two o'clock in the morning phone calls when he asked me to come down to A&E because his self-harm had gone too far. He wanted to talk about God and why things in this world were so evil, but he also wanted to talk about his drinking and drug bingeing sprees.

Offending other people in the pub was something he did so that he could get into a fight. One night he stood on our doorstep looking as if he had been wrestling with an ape. He was seething with rage and his clothes were torn. As we talked, it became clear that his appearance was self-inflicted from his deep frustration. He had done this to himself in the middle of a field while screaming at God.

Once we got to know him, the heated discussions eventually gave way to him opening up about his childhood experiences. He had been sexually abused, publicly ridiculed and brutally beaten at boarding school. To this day his family are supportive and caring but what upset him most was the masochistic cruelty of his teachers.

Jonathan did change over a period of about eighteen months. Sometimes he would have a meal with us or we visited him in his flat. Over time, we looked into various parts of Scripture that answered his questions about God or about himself and we would pray together. He eventually decided that he was like the Gadarene demoniac when we had first met, but was not like him now. Every step for Jonathan was a small painful step but it was a significant step forwards. And for many of us there is gradual repair but not necessarily complete healing.

Now, I am erring on the side of caution here. For some there can be a remarkable restoration. Most of the survivors I know make small but significant steps of progress on a lifetime journey. But it is so painfully slow that sometimes we are cheated into thinking we will never change and we are trapped in this miserable warped time-frame for life. I say, not so, even though for many years I have felt trapped. There are brand new beginnings. There is a new dawn.

I can never over-expect when Jesus is in control. He gives new beginnings like no one ever has nor can. If we will let him, he will walk with us on the journey and then, he will carry us when we cannot walk ourselves. God tells us: 'Behold, I am doing a new thing; now it springs forth, do you not perceive it? I will make a way in the wilderness and rivers in the desert'.[1]

Jonathan did not want slick answers. He wanted the truth. What we are saying here must not be taken as a slick answer to a complex problem. Steps of progress emerge from taking the journey seriously. What is meant by taking the journey seriously? There are two milestones on the journey of restoration that are significant points of progress. We may pass them many times before we get the long-term benefit; the benefit which comes from issues being left in the past, life being lived in the present, and the hope of a real life in the future. These two milestones are very much a part of journeying through the zones described in chapter 10 (Chart 2):

- Taking control and responsibility for the present and future journey gradually establishes a history past and a life in the future.[2]
- Maintaining safety and battling for the truth to hold onto, gains a life in the present.[3]

You hear people say, 'One day at a time' or 'Just one step at a time.' This is a realistic and solid expectation to have. Those steps are most significant when issues are being left in the past, life is being lived in the present, and we have the hope of a real life in the future.

'One Step Further' is a support group that we helped run for vulnerable women. One of the extraordinary women we had the privilege of working with came up with the name, and I love it because it is realistic. It has an expectancy that we are going forward, but just one step at a time. It also accepts that we are building on how far we have come already. It is healthy because each of us will take the steps we can take and be responsible for ourselves. We support each other with respect as equals in Christ. The past is behind and the future is ahead. Brand new beginnings is what we should expect. God promised a brand new beginning in the Lord Jesus and that happened to me when I was eighteen years old. Each day is a new day in which I receive steadfast love and never-ending mercy. Every day is a new beginning.

Having those two milestones as a working model gives us a realistic hope no matter what we are going through. In the first statement is the word 'gradually' and in the second statement 'gains'. It is slow and it can be painful. Sometimes our gains are so gradual we cannot see them and we feel that we are standing still. But we are standing! There can be an unexpected breakthrough on the journey when something fitted into place and that was thrilling. But these unexpected moments or new emotions often 'popped up' out of the routine of taking small and significant steps. Then there are the bad days or the dark depressing nights and we see ourselves slipping back. Be open and walk in the light at these times so that people can pray for you and with you.

Low times can be our best times to get close to God. We can be more open to learn from Him and gradually we take control and take responsibility. As we keep on doing this we battle to hold on to truth and to keep safe and secure. Like Jonathan, our history is left behind in the past and our future starts to look more promising. We enjoy extended times of being safe and, with God's truth in our lives, we find life has a new quality to it. The two milestones become the pattern of new beginnings in each new day.

New emotions, new personality, new freedom

'That energy is God's energy, and energy deep within you, God himself willing and working at what will give him the most pleasure.'

Paul in Philippians 2:13, *The Message*

'I am healing, a baby-step at a time.'

Survivor[1]

What are the possibilities for those who survive the evils of past abuse? What kind of future does a trauma sufferer have? These are tough questions that need realistic answers. There are possible outcomes that many survivors beginning their journey will think impossible. What I considered to be out of the question and beyond my dreams is now becoming possible.

Jesus said that He will make a new heaven and a new earth. For now, we will be imperfect on His earth but God intends to make us far better than we are now even on this earth. It is something He delights to do. Therefore we are told, 'continue to work out your salvation, for it is God who works in you to will and to act according to his good pleasure.'[2] Outcomes beyond our dreams become possible because God himself is at work in us to bring about what delights Him, as we follow Him.

What needs to be said again is that this must not be taken as a slick answer. In our communities are caring people who sow seeds of hope that grow in the rich soil of faith. Hope and faith are seriously lacking in those whose dreams and trust have been systematically destroyed. We need to be with people who, like Jesus, inspire hope and faith. The small shaky steps of faith give new confidence in possibilities. Hopes and dreams come from people like this to become an unexpected never-imagined delight.

Thank God that, until we find these people, we have a Friend whose love for us is stronger than death. Jesus shows us possibilities; He builds up our confidence in Him; He gives us a certain hope and dreams beyond all we ever thought we could expect. He brings us to a place where we can relate harmoniously with those we found impossible to relate to. He developed three things that I never expected to experience. They were new emotions, new personality and new freedoms. (Chart 4)

New Emotions

These can be sudden but more often are hardly noticeable being so gradual, like the strengthening of muscles over time. The old grim emotions which overshadowed and dominated everything are weakened by new positive emotions. One day I found a new joy. Where did that come from? The depression is not hanging over me as long as it used to and there is an increasing sense of hopefulness. Abandonment and hopelessness are no longer severe or as prolonged; but there is an expectancy and the Father's comfort to be worn like warm winter clothes. Thoughts of self-destruction are now very rare and brief. Perhaps it is because everything seemed so utterly grim that now the brightness of new emotions is so utterly pleasant. What is happening?

New pathways of thought eventually bring in new emotions. I read this last sentence over and over because it is true. Changed emotions are a side effect from a change in thinking. We do not change our thinking with the aim of achieving more healthy emotions but because it is right to think right. Another outstandingly helpful line Paul writes is, 'Finally brothers, whatever is true, whatever is noble, whatever is right, whatever is pure, whatever is lovely, whatever is admirable, if anything is excellent or praiseworthy, *think about such things*'.[3]

This change of thought patterns is pivotal in the gradual stop-start change in emotions. But there is another side to this which is significant for me, particularly when there are setbacks; when there are more stops than starts. Without doubt, an increasing intimacy with my Father God and with Jesus my Saviour have been at the core of all that has been happening. Jesus has met me in the depths and shown me how to cry out to Him so that I am lifted out of the grotty, grim, black sludge and given a solid foundation in Him that doesn't slip or slide every which-way.

CHART 4
Possible Outcomes considered Impossible

This must not be taken as a slick answer. It is not intended as a quick response. But it can be what emerges after time when the journey has been taken seriously

"For I know the plans I have for you, declares the Lord, plans to prosper you and NOT to harm you, plans to give you a hope and a future." Jer.29:11
"And we know that in ALL things God works for the good of those who love Him, who have been called according to his purpose." Rom.8:28

- Taking control and responsibility for the present and future journey gradually establishes a history PAST and a life in the FUTURE
- Maintaining safety and battling for the truth to hold on to these truths gains a life in the PRESENT (RL)

New Emotions	New Personality	New Freedom
Fun, laughter, joy Love in a truth spectrum – self-less, unconditional love (Agape) Peace that is beyond description Security, solidness, boldness, hopefulness New pathways of thought eventually bring in new emotions "When the act of telling the story is concluded the traumatic experience belongs in the past" Judith Hermon	New attitudes and characteristics are discovered or grow while some things of the old remain A different and truer identity is discovered. A move from victim to survivor and from survivor to victor/ thriver Taking fresh courage to choose the new road for the new journey Living in the Holy Spirit	Knowing the extent of God's forgiveness for others and for oneself Living within safe boundaries (Body, Mind and Environment) Experiencing the power of the cross to set us free from guilt, shame and everything that holds us back Enjoying the Holy Spirit setting us free and transforming us into Jesus' likeness
"forgetting what is behind and straining towards what is ahead" Phil.3:13 "whatever is true, whatever is noble, whatever is right, whatever is pure, whatever is lovely, whatever is admirable – if anything is excellent or praiseworthy – think about such things." Phil.4:8 "My peace I give you..." John 14:27 "..that they may have the full measure of my joy within them" John17:13	"And we all, who with unveiled faces contemplate the Lord's glory, are being transformed into his image with ever-increasing glory, which comes from the Lord, who is the Spirit." 2 Cor.3:18 "Don't you know that you yourselves are God's temple and that God's Spirit lives among you? .. for God's temple is sacred, and you together are that temple" 1Cor.3:16 cf. 6:11 "..the mind governed by the Spirit is life and peace." Romans 8:4,6	".forgive us our debts, as we also have forgiven our debtors." Matt.6:12 "..be transformed by the renewing of your mind." Rom.12:2 "I have been crucified with Christ and I no longer live, but Christ lives in me. The life I now live in the body, I live by faith in the Son of God, who loved me and gave himself for me." Gal.2:20 "if the Son sets you free, you will be free indeed" John 8:36

Fresh ways of thinking have then become trusted and depended on. Truth and companionship have been at the core of my mental hygiene. This is the crucial fight; to take hold of what is true, the truths the Lord has given in His word, and reject what are lies. One example of this are the days when I feel like a leper; an untouchable—someone who is separated out from the community and isolated because of their disease. My mind tells me that this is not how God sees me but I still feel like a leper. But I then get hold of a different thought. Jesus touched the lepers and healed them. He has no problem with lepers. He loves them just like He loves everyone. That fresh thought brings in new emotions.

Then there is also a watershed—a point at which eventually the past is left in the past and I have turned my back on it. When things try to creep back again they must be put back where they belong. For me this would include particular people or experiences. Judith Herman describes the watershed like this: 'When the action of telling the story has come to its conclusion, the traumatic experience truly belongs in the past.'[4] We leave the past in the past and now have hope to build our ambitions for a different future.

So what else is happening now that is different? There is a new strength from understanding the traumatic experience and seeing it from God's perspective. The perspective that David and Joseph found[5] and we develop from journeying in the Scriptures. With this strength, I start to leave the threatening triggers and bad emotions, such as rejection, in the past and challenge them when they invade the present. I can now see the threats coming that remind me of the past and more often (but not always) manage the triggers. The struggle to handle feelings of rejection and abandonment was new territory but made a great difference. We look at this in chapter 21.

It is obvious to me now, that abandonment has been one of the biggest triggers and has wrongly coloured so many issues. The core of the traumatic experience and accompanying triggers are like a faulty, failing heart that needs replacing by a working heart. Isn't that a bit dramatic or radical? Yes! This is what new thought patterns do in giving us a more reliable brain. When, for example, there is a trigger of rejection instead of accepting the emotion I now challenge it. If something is said to me that hurts, I feel free now to ask if this is what was actually meant or, to say politely, what you have just said is unkind or hurtful. Challenging your own negative emotions can be difficult at first. But it does lead to positive experiences which build hope and confidence as you take more control of the triggers and the emotions. The ongoing battle to replace negative emotions is gradually paid off by healthy productive new emotions.

New Personality

Can this be possible? It has to be. Simply because we are taking back the ground in our life that was torn from us. Restoring aspects of our childhood that belonged to us.

One sunny day I was enjoying a walk to the shops. I began to think about what God had been doing. Why should I not be proud (not a good word but you know what I mean) of what He has been making me to be—why be ashamed? I began to lift my chin up and walk more upright. Why shouldn't I be bold and strong?

Perhaps it is still early days for you on your journey, but eventually I hope that a new day will dawn for you. Because when God does His work in our life, He makes us new and this has a significant impact on our personality. It is not that we suddenly become an entirely different person, but it is the work of ongoing grace to bring ongoing change. The images of the old lifeless stony heart made alive and the 'new creation'[6] are central to our spiritual experience. The new birth is just the beginning. God continues His work in us as we have seen already, and with our co-operation and a focus on Jesus, gradual and radical change is possible. He sends great grace as our personal trainer.[7] We will look at this more closely in the next section.

The reality is that much of the time this appears to us to be very slow because God's new creation is living inside a very human body. New attitudes and characteristics grow while some things of the old remain. The old attitudes can be dominant if our human side is our focus. The new life is dominant if our new steps in the Holy Spirit are our focus.[8] This is complex and challenging enough for someone who has not been abused. For the survivor, it can be a leap to the moon because it comes back again to trust, and daring to trust when the past comes back to haunt us. Learning to trust where trust has been so terminally betrayed is like learning to walk all over again. And to begin with, it is all up hill.

How do we trust again? Well, we have already been very courageous to live the way we have lived. People have let us down badly and we may think that God has let us down too. We are a survivor. Fresh courage is needed. We are already a fighter, battling through each day. Some of that fighter in us has to take a courageous step and make a decision to keep going on a new journey. It is like a fork in the road when we make decisions like this. This is something we have to decide for ourselves.

The best starting point I found was discovering another world in God; living by the Holy Spirit and keeping in step with Him. Living this new life is like going from black and white to full colour. It is another life and that is a great incentive. This is a decision only we can make. I started to choose not to go down the lower, darker road, which had become the easier option. Taking the choice to drink, thinking that I was deadening the pain, was the easier road. Retreating when confronted by a dominant person or exploding when I was reminded about past experiences, were the easier roads to take.

For most of my life I have believed in the power of prayer as calling on the One who has all power to bring about His will. Never in my life, since the early days of living with the Lord, have I experienced the power of constant prayer. Whether we call it devoted prayer or continuous prayer doesn't really matter. What matters is crying out to my Father in heaven and keep on crying out to Him until I change. Living in the Spirit and real prayer are establishing a new trust.

A different and truer identity is discovered as we move from victim to survivor and from survivor to thriver. It is not perfection yet, so it is truer to say that I live far less as a victim and more time, but not all the time, as a thriver. And I thank God that the difference is as dramatic as some of the events in the past have been. It is tough at times to choose the new road. Choosing it again and again (and especially after failing), will lead to major changes that will thrill you because you are choosing to walk with God. He is the One who makes the greatest changes in our personality to bring us in line with His original design for us before the abuse happened. 'the old has gone, the new has come'.[9] And God is committed to continuing this. Our new personality is inseparable from a new freedom.

New Freedom

Woooohooooo! Whoooheeeee! have become new expressions! Well, sometimes. Where the Spirit of the Lord is, there is freedom.[10] Where the

Lord in His might and power releases us from the grinding iron fist of sin and its related guilt and shame, we can fly into His presence. God's grace and love are more powerful than all the guilt and shame. In the power of the cross, grace and love set us free from guilt (what I have done) and shame (what I have become) to become increasingly like God.

We must keep saying this: the abuse we suffered is not our sin. God condemns the perpetrator who committed the sin against you. We read that He constantly sides with the victims and deals with the perpetrators.[11] So, when I look at all that He has released me from, it includes all the things that I have personally done wrong, that which is genuinely my sin. It also includes the hold of other people's sin for which I am not personally responsible. Any of this may still be tripping me up or holding me back.

If we were to surface from being under water where we cannot breathe, into fresh air, the change would be noticeable and obvious. Living under water without God and then being brought to the surface to live on the land where we live and breathe God, is completely liberating. From there in our new life we learn to be in orbit with God rising up into His presence on the wings of an eagle.[12] This is not a mere fantasy for super-spiritual Olympians, but the new life in the Holy Spirit that God births into all His children. I need to be constantly reminded of this because I forget so quickly. But please hear me as I say this again: all this is more accessible and acceptable for those who have not been abused. God can do miracles, but for some of us, for the sake of His own glory, He chooses a journey of gradual transformation.

The barriers a survivor faces seem mountainous and impossible. The overwhelming feeling is that this freedom we are talking about is something that others can experience but not me as a survivor. If I think about this, my conclusion is that I must be as content as possible living with the pain of past sin and its present effects on my life. I do not have the strength to do anything else but to resign myself to captivity. Freedom from sin and from its effects is not for me. Is that how you want to live?

On the contrary, this blows me away: God is doing a transforming work in me to make me like His Son, Jesus. Why does it say, 'Where the Spirit of the Lord is, there is freedom'? Paul is telling us in 2 Corinthians 3:4–18 why his message is profoundly different from the teachings of the Rabbi's. This is why: 'where the Spirit of the Lord is, there is freedom.' That is fantastic news. This freedom, like a priceless jewel, is a many facetted freedom. The Holy Spirit sets us free from a hard heart against God, from spiritual death, from blindness to the great news that Jesus came to rescue us, from guilt and condemnation. The presence of the Holy Spirit in our lives sets us free but we can't stop there. If we do, we miss God's ultimate reason or purpose for doing this.

This is truly amazing; we are now being transformed into God's likeness which He created for humans before Adam and Eve messed up in the Garden of Eden. We are set free to fly into the arms of God and gaze up at Jesus which over time brings transformation into His likeness. The word 'transformed' is the same word from which we get the word 'metamorphosis': a complete change into something brand new, just like the chrysalis into a butterfly. A stunning transformation. God sets us free to become like Himself; a transformation which He continues in us. This keeps us encouraged. It is also how Paul kept going no matter what came against him, and it will help us not to lose heart. I am being changed by the Holy Spirit to become like Jesus. Oh, what a new freedom. Isn't this significant for survivors to become thrivers?

Freedom begins from two starting points. The first is when I know that I am totally forgiven because of what Jesus has done for me and not by what I do for Him. The second is in knowing the sin blame does not rest on me for what happened when I was a child. I have had to tell myself this and then retell myself so that I genuinely believed it. Does God hold you accountable for all that abuse you were involved with? Does God really blame the child? That is a most important question.

We are talking about freedom. We need to be clear. There are many kinds of freedom but only one true spiritual freedom that is ours only in the Lord Jesus Christ. Only He, of all the prophets, is God. It begins when we hold onto what He has done and hold onto what He has said. It increases, and is greater in its impact, as we hold onto what we learn from what He has said. That is His promise. 'If the Son sets you free, you are free indeed.'[13] Wooooheeeee!! I should really say that more often!

On the Edge of Heaven or the Edge of Hell

'Birds born in a cage think flying is an illness.'

Alexandro Jodorowsky[1]

'You intended to harm me, but God intended it for good to accomplish what is now being done, the saving of many lives.'

Joseph in Genesis 50:20

'If you are going through hell, keep going.'[2]

'It isn't the mountains ahead to climb that wear you out; it's the pebble in your shoe.'

Mohamed Ali

Is this the point where we have a happy ending and walk into a beautiful sunset? In this chapter, we look at what it can be like to come through from restoration to transformation and also what it takes to hold on to a better future. But I imagine that there might be some unanswered questions. Why has this taken so long to sort out? How can a Christian and a church leader's life and marriage be this damaged? And why did God allow this to happen?

I do wonder sometimes why the Lord didn't restore me sooner. One answer to these questions that satisfies me is what Joseph said to his abusive brothers. 'You intended to harm me, but God intended it *for good* to accomplish what is now being done, the saving of many lives.' God works everything together for our good. I do not fully understand this but I do hold onto His higher purpose.

While I was visiting Ghana, I was taken to see a slave fort near Takoradi called Cape Coast Castle. Here slaves were pressed into small dungeons waiting to go through the 'gate of no return' to be transported and sold as possessions of another human. The conditions they were kept in were horrific; the life ahead for them unspeakable. Can you imagine what it was like when slave trading was abolished and slaves were given their rightful freedom? Harriet Tubman was born into slavery. She escaped and subsequently made some thirteen missions to rescue approximately seventy enslaved families and friends, 'the saving of many lives.' This is what she said and I think she is referring to her new freedom: 'I looked at my hands to see if I was the same person. There was such a glory over everything. The sun came up like gold through the trees, and I felt like I was in heaven.'[3]

After all this time, one outcome is a glorious freedom that is hard to describe. Jesus gave the Samaritan woman her freedom. Then there was the Gaderene demoniac, the paralytic on his mat, the woman who washed Jesus's feet, and many others who, when they met with Jesus, were set wonderfully free. In a similar way, though more gradual I can join the list and like Harriet can say, 'When Jesus gave me spiritual freedom there was His glory over everything and I felt like I was visiting heaven.'

Originally, I thought that the final chapter would be about the real grit of living in 'survivor' mode. Something like: once a victim but now an adamant survivor and tasting what it is like to be a 'thriver'. Well, that is no longer my experience. Survivor mode is something I had settled down into like a cosy couch potato; not through laziness but through being realistic about the long haul of restoration. Now, completely unexpectedly, like waking up from a nightmare, I am living much of the time as a thriver. I really didn't think there would be even a hint of a happy ending but now there is. We'll leave out the walk into the sunset! But I am singing along regularly to songs like 'Thriver' by Casting Crowns.

> 'We know we were made for so much more
> Than ordinary lives.
> It's time for us to more than just survive
> We were made to thrive.'[4]

For many years, like most survivors, I have moved around the phases. Some days firmly back in 'Safety and Security' and it is solid and reassuring. Then there are weeks in 'The Fight' and it's all rejoicing, conquering, praise and I am up for most things! Then something comes along and it takes me to the depths of 'Remembrance and Mourning' again. These are painful, depressing times where I struggle to hold on to hope, to see the positive instead of the negative. Phone calls are made to trusted friends who tell me how it really is or I go for a drive by myself so that I can have a praise CD on full blast and stand in God's presence. Oh, the sweet times of 'Reconnection' with Jesus and with others.

The important thing was to move in the right direction and at times I moved quicker than I had expected. What I was taking on board escalated. Down times have become fewer and further apart. Good times are bigger, better and more significant. One reason for this is I meet with fellow survivors regularly. It is important for me to be a realist and to be as open and as honest as it is right or appropriate to be, which is a challenge in itself. I have learnt the hard way that it is damaging to open up and walk in the light with some people. It takes a long time to know that a person can really be trusted because they are godly, dependable and sit alongside you not taking the high moral ground. This person will remind you of Jesus. Fellow survivors teach, remind and encourage me. Much of the stuff of restoration cannot be done alone, unless you are a superhero. Another reason is remembering that my (spiritual) birthright is life in the Holy Spirit; a life set free from addictions.

Today is amazing and I am still trying to understand it. If someone had told me four years ago that this is where I would be I could not have accepted it, even though I wanted it with all my heart. Finally, I have a release, like a bird from a cage and the freedom is out of this world. It is like living on the outskirts of heaven instead of the outskirts of hell.

The wilderness journey is coming to an end and all that I have gained through it has strengthened me. I am free. The Lord has brought down barriers in His time, in His way and by His power. What are some of the parts of this journey that have brought me through to being the 'thriver'?

- letting the secret out and disarming the hijackers (whether people, thoughts etc).
- deeper insights of God in His nature.
- a healthy awareness of the phases in a survivor's journey.
- understanding how what happened in the past effected me in the present.

- •accepting that what happened was a sin against me and was not my responsibility.
- learning to be patient and reasonable with myself.
- mental hygiene (see p ??????) so that my mind is feeding on what is true and realistic.
- realising the value of journeying companions and that this could not be done alone.
- being part of a healing Church community with other survivors.
- appreciating some of the significant gains alongside the losses.
- knowing that things were going to get worse before getting better.
- enjoying an emerging strength, confidence and new life from the journey.
- standing in the armour of Christ against the onslaught of the enemy to stand solid.
- having a purpose to live for that invests in other people.
- emphasising the positives to shift away from auto-negative.

The grace, mercy, truth and love that is always there cannot be overlooked. I thank God for support from fellow travellers and they are vital. But the real difference is down to what I do and the steps that I take with my Jesus. That is heaven! What holds me is what God supplies directly or through others. Family, church friends, and health professionals can unknowingly be significant channels of grace, mercy, love and truth. But ultimately: 'It's all about Jesus and not about me.' I have wanted to shout this in church sometimes.

We can get so caught up with, 'Me, me, me' that we lose sight of Jesus. We fall into the age-old trap of thinking that we set the tone; it's what we have done, what we are, and what we try to do to sort it out. It is all about Jesus. He sets the tone by all He has done and all that He is. It is grace upon grace, mercy upon mercy, truth upon truth, love upon love. My deepest need is to have a better vision of Jesus—who He is and what He has done. At times of feeling weak and useless I get up and say 'Jesus, we do this together.' and He always does his part.

What is a Thriver like?

My all-time favourite parable is the father and his two prodigal sons. Here Jesus is trying to get across to us what God is like, the contrast of what it is like to be treated by the 'Big Brother' (not pleasant!) and what happens when we turn around and go back to our Father God. I keep going back to what Jesus taught here because I can identify with it.[5]

What is a thriver like? I think he is just like the younger son who is now in his father's house. He has met a side to his father that he has never met before. After he messed up and was at the end of himself, his plan was to go back to his father, confess and volunteer to be an undeserving house slave. Think of that—a volunteer slave! But when he confesses, his father sweeps him into the house before he has chance to make his offer. In the father's mind, he is never going to be a slave but a son. A thriver lives as an honoured son and heir in his heavenly Father's house.[6]

It seems to have taken me a lifetime to understand what it is like to be in my Father's house as His honoured son. This is the extreme opposite to where a life of abuse is. It is the very place where God wants us to be. This son who has journeyed home is now wearing the best suit in the house—a new identity from God; a ring is now on his finger—a new authority from God; and sandals on his feet—a sign of sonship. Slaves did not wear sandals. When he looks down on a bad day he will not see bare feet! These gifts are a constant reminder of the unconditional love his Father has shown him, that his back is towards a buried past and he is facing a glorious future. He can no longer abuse himself, nor will he be abused by his 'Big Brother'. That is the journey I have taken. The more I realise what God is like in contrast to the 'Big Brother' the more I thrive.

Like a war veteran or crash victim, survivors are understandably frustrated, upset, and disturbed from the wreckage of their past and addition of blunders or bad experiences since then. To move forward we need to find fresh ways of seeing things so that by repeating these, we reprogram our minds.[7]

As I write this, Sue and I are about to celebrate forty years of marriage. But a few months ago we were tripped up by a minor tsunami. For six years we have been trying to repair the damage of the past and we have successfully rebuilt aspects of our relationship. So much has changed and we are better for it. Our mistake was to look too closely into our responses.

Progress on a journey of recovery from PTSD involves coming to terms with the past and processing personal developments. Bitter experience has shown us that improving our relationships is different and does not come from trying to fix the past. It is far more effective to build a future. We accept that we were not on the same page in the past but we can be in the future.

Building for a different future places the focus on the best in us. Analysing the past looks at our failures by emphasising wrong actions and can apportion blame even while struggling to understand one another's point of view. This can quickly lead into pressing one another's buttons which escalates an avalanche of more complex problems, hurts, fears and failures. There is a right time for admitting mistakes, asking forgiveness, and establishing boundaries. We have found great benefit from moving on from this so that we keep going forwards: 'If you want a taste of freedom, keep going.'

This is a powerful encouragement that Jesus gives this to His people (at the church in Philadelphia) so that they can move forward: 'See, I have placed before you an open door that no one can shut. I know that you have little strength, yet you have kept my word and have not denied my name'.[8] Jesus speaks this over a Christian community that have little that is impressive. They have a reputation for being weak and are overshadowed by Satanic opposition. But Jesus sees an outstanding thing that He values. They may be weak but they are loyal to Him and they persevere. They may be in a hellish place but they keep on going! These, Jesus says, will go on to become 'a pillar in the temple of my God'.

I have lost count of the number of survivors I have met from a variety of tragedies who are just like this. They may have a pebble in their shoe but they keep going and they inspire me to do the same. To these, Jesus gives 'a door standing open' and 'What he opens no one can shut and what he shuts no one can open.'[9] What is this open door?

For Paul it was always an opportunity to move into a new phase of work with Jesus. But it could also mean the open door we have into heaven now and for eternity. Why not both? Like these Christians, we have pressed through so much suffering. There is now in front of us an open door of opportunity to work with Jesus and become a solid, dependable functioning member of His community. That is His promise to those who keep going through their hellish experiences.

Where I am going from here?

Today is a brand new moment without the mess and filth of the past staining me. Instead, it is the refreshing, cleansing and building thoughts from new patterns of thinking that influence me. The Lord has made me to be a new creation by His salvation. That is where all my thinking needs to be right now. To move forward, my mind must be set solid in the concrete foundation of new thinking for a new life, motivated by the taste of freedom he gives: 'Forgetting what is behind and straining toward what is ahead.'[10]

I can see my past as a closed door because I have journeyed through and between the phases to a point of conclusion. The hell-like pain and grief of the process has lessened and I am, as sure as hell, not going to get stuck here. I have kept going and am now at a point where I can turn my back on this hell. In every sense heaven is in front of me! This is what I need the healing community to remind me of. This I can do with Jesus because he says so![11]

One of my biggest problems in the past, perhaps the biggest of all, was that my head was left in a mess. Peter tells us that in the light of all that God has done 'prepare your minds for action'.[12] I'm drawing a line in the sand and it reads, 'No more mess but clean-truth thinking.' Here are some of my clean truths.

- I will be defined by what the Lord says about me and not by what I do, nor by my past. Nor will I be defined by other people. I am thankful for everyone who has been a productive influence, but stand against any form of exploitation.
- I am in control of every part of my life (this includes feelings, thoughts, actions, decisions and more). No one else on earth controls me but there is One in heaven who is in perfect control and is loving and gracious in all His dealings with me.
- I am invited to sit in the highest place in the whole universe: right beside my Jesus. He is the victorious One over sin and death and I side with Him as one of His 'more than conquerors'.
- I have times of great fun and enjoyment and will have, even in times that are bleak. When I look for joy I will find it.
- I belong to God and am a man of God. In myself I have limited ability. In God, His abilities in me are unlimited. In myself I have limited strength. In God, my strength is unlimited. I can do what I

need to do. I may at times lack the resources but I know Someone who has them!
- I am what I am because this is the way God has made me. I will celebrate all that is good and productive and depend on Him to change the not so good without putting myself down or beating myself up.
- I press forward now and with God's grace will be useful to Him and to others.

The incessant niggle from the pebble in my shoe is not what it used to be. It may be that it has reduced in size. But it is certain that I have found a place in my shoe to keep it so that it is far less of a pain! This is because I have now closed off the past and opened a new future and I will stand in this new thought process again and again, so that it is established.

The power to change comes from co-operating with the Lord in the renewal of our minds and particularly our motivations, attitudes, desires, opinions and ambitions. Romans 12:12 shows us this: 'Do not conform any longer to the pattern of this world, but be transformed by the renewing of your mind.' No one can do this for us but the Lord is in partnership with us. It is down to us to see transformation after our restoration. A restoration that comes from reprogramming our thinking and keeping hold of this mental hygiene for a new life. Before us is 'an open door that no one can shut.'[13] Thank God for His ways into transformation for a productive future as we keep going forwards.

Chapter 22

A Word to Supporters

'Carry each other's burdens, and in this way you will fulfil the law of Christ.'

Galatians 6:2

'Over the years, we have seen the most effective recovery by our girls take place in the context of relationships. We have the credibility to help girls and women only when we offer them authentic ongoing connection. After all, it is only through our relationship with Jesus that we are restored to the Father.'

Mary Frances Bowley[1]

Are you a fixer? That is me, for sure. Something in the temperament of some of us loves to fix things. Are you reading this book with someone in mind; someone who has been abused who you want to help fix to make their life all better? Please, don't. There are a number of reasons why I caution you not to, and they are all important.

Control is a major issue and, whether you are aware of it or not, if you begin to take control of their life you will more than likely add to their abuse.

Some forms of counselling and caring necessarily carry an element control. So this needs to be put clearly. A survivor of child abuse has been controlled by an abuser in many different ways. Some were very subtle forms of manipulation while others were blatant dominance. Now, at whatever point they are on their journey, it is essential that they have all the control for themselves. The most well-meaning people can get their satisfaction and meaning in life from helping others. But what can happen is a 'needy person' becomes a personal project and personal satisfaction comes from controlling them. This has been called 'Christian pimping'. A well-meaning organisation can also do this. Taking control of their life alongside them may seem the right option, but it could actually traumatise them all over again. It will at the least slow down their restoration.

Most of us will be aware that the issues for a person traumatised in childhood are many and complex. A little knowledge can be damaging. At a seminar on Childhood Trauma, the lecturer ended by warning us not to try this ourselves without further training. I am so glad that she said this as I, with many others, have been halted in our progress by well-meaning but harmful advice.

In reality, what we all want to see is survivors on a journey of restoration. It is a powerful element in the journey when the survivor is given all the control for that journey by those who walk alongside them. Support is invaluable and so we must learn the difference between a controlling help and a non-controlling support. Some of our best guidelines come from Jesus' interaction with the most vulnerable, and the definitions in 1 Corinthians 13 of God's love in action. Here we find 'non-controlling support' or an 'authentic ongoing connection.'

Being alongside Survivors

Paul gave to the Galatian Christians this workable principle: they were to be alongside each other and get under another's burden to carry it with them.[2] He demonstrates that this is what a life of love in the Spirit looks like. The mature and experienced, the 'spiritual', are to be there to 'restore gently' the beleaguered, troubled or hard-pressed brother or sister. Then they would be doing a great job because they will be doing it like the greatest burden bearer—Jesus.

My driving instructor was clearly knowledgeable and experienced but not demanding or overpowering. He handed over the car to me to drive and sat next to me relaxing in his slippers! Little by little he suggested adjustments to my bad driving habits as we journeyed together. Sometimes Sue will buy the ingredients for a meal and then take it to one of our dear women and they will cook it. Many of them do not eat. They will take their drugs and strong coffee with many sugars, but not food; they therefore can get quite emaciated. Sue watches as they do all the cooking and then eats what they have cooked. She never says, 'Snap out of it. Leave it in the past' or 'Behave' or 'Be healed'. The best work from charities or individuals can hold back survivors if they do not get the 'burden bearing' right.

The best role I can think of is one of being a servant-facilitator. A facilitator is not a leader and a servant is definitely not a master or a controller. A servant-facilitator is rather like my driving instructor in the passenger seat allowing the learner driver to take all the controls. It doesn't take much imagination to see how scary that can be (perhaps for both of them!), but it is most definitely empowering for the learner. Every illustration breaks down at some point and this one fails by assuming that the driving instructor has all the knowledge and the learner passively learns. Well, the servant-facilitator soon finds that they learn more and receive more from the survivor than they ever were aware of giving. What a thrilling journey.

Let's take this to the most effective level. It is a journey with the Lord. What they gain from me will only go so far. As a servant-facilitator I want them to receive from the Lord for themselves. That will take the survivor far further on their journey. I must remember that in reality it is the Lord in the passenger seat and I am in the back.

Something I often tell myself is to see others with the eyes of Jesus, listen to them with the ears of Jesus, think of them with the mind of Jesus and surround them with arms of Jesus. Surely in this way we enter into Christ's own mission, love like him and fulfil his ultimate, highest law.[3] There is absolutely no room in me for a superior attitude or thinking that a person is more sinful. The playing field has been levelled. 'For there is no distinction, for all have sinned and fall short of the glory of God.'[4] That includes all of us. We need genuinely to believe this and live it. A critical or judgmental attitude in me will never work. When a survivor catches a whiff of this attitude they run a mile and stay away. To my sadness I have seen this happen.

Let me pass on a few quick pointers from what we have found helpful in growing to be servant-facilitators?

- At all times look at a survivor as your equal. Do not judge them.
- Learn to listen with your heart. Do not jump in with solutions.
- Talk to the Lord about them often. Do not talk much to others about them.
- Be realistic, truthful and sincere. Do not make promises or give false hope or plastic answers or sweet platitudes like, 'Just trust

the Lord!' Remember that trust is a massive step, and that includes trusting God.

- Be unshockable, if at all possible. There can be extreme ups and downs; start-stops; a little progress and then disastrous sliding back; you might be appreciated and then hated.
- Compassion and sincerity go a long way. Be loving and truth-filled particularly when criticised or verbally attacked. Remember it's a cross we carry not a throne.
- Truth from our lives, mental hygiene, and life in the Spirit, need to be seen before they are heard. Right attitudes and responses speak as loudly as wrong ones. Is this why Jesus began his teachings here?[5]
- You don't need to be perfect and you certainly don't need to fear making mistakes. We all do and that is how we learn.
- Work in a team so that you do not become depended upon (or worse you depend on them), and so that you yourself have the support and wise counsel from others.[6]

Having said all this, spiritual communities of Jesus' disciples are an oasis of healing. At the right time, the right church is where he does a great work in each of us.

A word for the Church: heaven's heroes

> 'I tell you the truth, anyone who has faith in me will do what I have been doing. He will do even greater things than these, because I am going to the Father.'
>
> John 14:12

> 'Get on fire for God and men will come and see you burn.'
>
> John Wesley

> 'God's heart breaks for the twenty-seven million men, women and children worldwide who are trapped in some form of slavery'
>
> Louie Giglio

If I was only allowed to say one sentence from the front of the church it would be this. 'Keep Jesus central and keep what Jesus did central, then we will be doing what Jesus is doing today.'

What the people who I meet with need is unconditional love and genuine encouragement from God. Unfortunately, looking back I know that I have wasted too much time on projects and events that produced little fruit. This spurs me on to keep Jesus and people, not projects, central; in this way, my remaining days will be precious in heaven's eyes. Because it is people who are precious in heaven's eyes. God invests himself in the broken, the despised and the destitute. So will I.

What do you think of when you hear Jesus saying, 'Open your eyes and look at the fields! They are ripe for harvest'? What is it that Jesus sees and points out to us? Who are ripe for harvest? Why are the disciples so surprised?[1] Let's look at the last question first. The disciples return to find Jesus talking with a woman and he is a Rabbi. One of the many rules Rabbi's had was, 'Let no one talk with a woman in the street, no, not with his own wife.'[2] Jesus is a Jew and He is speaking to, what they would see as, a 'scum-dog-Samaritan woman'. A woman from a tribe who are now unclean because way back in their history some of the Jews had intermarried. It has therefore become their tradition not go anywhere near them. Another rule was not to drink from the same cup, otherwise they would make themselves unclean. In addition to this, he is the Messiah and she is a well-known sinner.

Do we see the picture here? Jesus crosses social barriers, ignores taboos, and breaks traditions. He crosses the bridge into her life just as He crossed the bridge into our world. Is this the Jesus you know? The only One who has spiritual water, crosses the bridge to meet the spiritually thirsty *where they are.*[3] But the disciples were astonished. 'What is He doing now? Haven't we got better things to do than talk to a Samaritan woman?'

The next thing they see is not just one of these rejected, social outcasts, and a known despised sinner, but a whole crowd of them coming towards them! '*They* are ripe for harvest.' The grain harvest is four months away, but the soul harvest is ready now, Jesus did not train his disciples to ask people to cross the bridge into the disciples' world but to see, go, and cross the bridge into their world. It is a crowd of Samaritans that Jesus opens his disciples' eyes to see. He is training them to be heaven's heroes.

How effective is our church at crossing the bridge into a different world without making the mistakes that have been made in the past? Have we begun to look differently and hear Jesus with fresh ears when he said, 'Open your eyes and look at the fields! They are ripe for harvest.' Is there some other way I can say this? Is it possible that visitors, who have bravely crossed the threshold into a church gathering, find themselves frowned at or ignored, or even spoken to in an unloving judgmental way? Yet there are over two thousand one hundred verses in our Bible which tell us how our Father views the destitute; how he wants justice for them and what he wants us to do.

Some sincere Christians may not get this, perhaps because it is so far outside their own experience and understanding: 'Christian survivors should not be like this. They should not behave in this way. It's too emotional', is how we may think, as if this is a disease that should have been healed at spiritual birth. Yet there are others at Church who see the condition of survivors as a journey of change and accept them where they are. We are different and have challenges. Let's celebrate and accept our differences.

It is horrible to pluck up courage and go to church but then to be met by people's unapproving glances; to know that Jesus has transformed you on the inside but on the outside you do not meet the church's standard. For some survivors, their experience of church has put them off going and, even though they would like to, it is now out of the question. How can we, as God's communities, get this right in the future?

For a moment let us look at the woman who made a spectacle of herself over Jesus.[4] She lavishly pours perfume, worth hundreds of pounds, on Jesus; she cries so much that she can wash his feet; she plants kisses on His feet; she uses her hair as a towel! Is there anything that Jesus experienced that was as gushy, demonstrative and emotional? Her emotional eruption was wildly extreme—and Jesus loved it and interprets it for all those who objected: 'Therefore I tell you, her sins, which are many, are forgiven; for she loved much. But he who is forgiven little, loves little.' She really understands personal forgiveness and Jesus embraces another life devastated by sin. Should we not do as Jesus did?

There are two things that prepare us, as the church, to cross the bridge into Jesus' harvest:

1. Seeing how God regards the abused and then expects his people to act.

> 'O Lord, you are my God ... You have been a refuge for the poor, a refuge for the needy in distress, a shelter from the storm and a shade from the heat'.[5]

> 'If you spend yourselves on behalf of the hungry and satisfy the needs of the oppressed, then your light will arise in the darkness'.[6]

> 'Blessed is he who has regard for the weak; the Lord delivers him in times of trouble'.[7]

2. Seeing how the Lord trained his disciples.

They were to have a special care for the poor and not disregard them to favour the rich.[8]

They were to let sinners get close up to Jesus. The disciples saw first-hand the attitude of Simon the Pharisee and, in contrast, what Jesus' heart was like with a notorious sinner.[9]

They were to give their best workers to care for the widows. These had to be known 'to be full of the Spirit and wisdom'.[10]

They were to understand that who they served defined their true spirituality and that their good works proved the authenticity of their faith.[11]

What is the Lord expecting from His disciples? What marks out heaven's heroes? Surely there are at least these two things.

They Share God's heart for the destitute

Psalm 82:1–4 is a cry from God's people in Israel who were weak and were being mistreated. Wouldn't this be a song sung by the first groups of Christians for the same reason? Shouldn't this be our song today? A song that cries out to God for justice and also propels us into doing all we can to bring justice. Let us ask the Lord to open our eyes and see what walking with survivors involves. To walk alongside others as Jesus did is inspired, directed and sustained by understanding something of God's heart.

Jesus did tell the destitute to come to *him*. He also told his disciples that he would build his church. We know that he told his disciples to go into all the world to make disciples. Jesus invested in people. He seemed to spend more time training His team than on anything else. He then took the baton of his mission and passed it on to them—and to us.

Let's get it right. Our role is not to build up our church or our mission or project, but to make disciples of Jesus. Just as our role is not to bring the destitute to ourselves, but allow them to come to Jesus. God's heart for the destitute is a heart with purpose and that is to be training followers or disciples of Jesus. Without discipleship, our heart and purpose not only falls short of God's intention; it is disobedience to His clear instruction. Heaven's heroes delight in making disciples so that unconditional love is matched with purposeful hands-on training.

What is it we want to give survivors instead of glib statements? Isn't it this: we want them to know what it is to receive his gift of grace into the very centre of their unexplainable pain? They need nothing less than his power and anointing which he administers; the life-transforming truth they see in us as living Bibles. This is what he came to do. This is his work that is now made our work. It is a spiritual work done by the Holy Spirit as Jesus' own mission. It is a long journey of making disciples of Jesus—his way.

They join God at work through His Church

I can imagine that some, perhaps many, will think, 'Well what you have said lets me off the hook because I am certainly not one of the best or one of the gifted.' 1 Corinthians 12:22 tells us: 'those parts of the body that seem weaker are indispensable.' Why? Could it be because it is not the loudest, boldest, up-front gifts that God sees as the most significant? I suspect that in God's order it is the quiet, gentle, peripheral people who are the best to be alongside survivors who are on a journey of restoration.

Alice's story shows us the effectiveness of a quiet behind-the-scenes work:

'I was put in a care home and later as a teenager was raped. I've needed to spend time in psychiatric hospitals because I used to go wild and just couldn't cope. I was homeless in London for years. There were two Christian couples who at different times took me into their homes and showed me how much Jesus loves me. They help me with shopping and sorting out my home. I love to pray with them. My wild episodes have become less and less, and I haven't needed to go into hospital for three years. It's nice to go to church from time to time, but I find it hard because people look at me and that makes me feel different. But Jesus has done so much in my life and has changed me so I am not the same as I was.'

We talk to Alice on the phone almost every day and she continues to see her precious Jesus do wonderful things, but she still cannot go to church. That is partly how she is, but it is also how she has been put off by her experiences at church.

Let us not miss this vital part of God's design for His people. A major chunk of time in the church family could be spent trying to sort out problems or issues between people. My Bible tells me that the real struggle is not between people at all.[12] If that's what all my energy and time are absorbed with then I've completely missed the point and I have fallen into the trap of ineffectiveness. My ineffectiveness keeps our real enemy happy. What makes us, as God's people, really effective is standing upright in the mighty power of our risen Lord Jesus, fully dressed in His armour and praying and then going. God says that he works through his Church. And in case you are asking 'Which Church?' That is answered in chapter 2:19–22 of Ephesians.

God speaks peace and life, releasing prisoners captured by sin and bound by their brokenness. But what are His people doing? Could it be that we have been subtly distracted, working flat out to keep a religious clubhouse or a church programme going? Sleep walking through worship marathons? Blinkered by our teaching schedule or five-year plan? But God has decreed that He will work through His people, making them to be heaven's heroes.

These heroes go beyond giving or praying or doing a few good turns that satisfy their own conscience. They are tired of their own schedules and ambitions and are passionate about following what God is doing. These heroes have been captured by the cry from captured hearts and it motivates all that they do. They have heard the call of the Prince of Peace and have taken up the baton he passed on to his disciples: 'Go therefore and make disciples of all nations (every people group), baptising them in the name of the Father and of the Son and of the Holy Spirit, (it doesn't stop there) teaching them to observe or obey all or everything that I have commanded you'.[13]

The saints, the disciples of Jesus, have the baton, and they are not in a sprint to persuade as many 'nice people' as possible to keep chairs or pews warm on a Sunday. They are on a prayer marathon to see God release dead people from a prison-grave and from being held as captives by an evil power.

Our Father's heart is for the poor. For obvious reasons, the widows and orphans were the most vulnerable when the Bible was written. They could not defend themselves and the Lord Almighty stood in for them: 'He defends the cause of the fatherless and the widow, and loves the alien, giving him food and clothing'.[14]

God gives clear instructions to His people about how they are to treat the vulnerable, and severely warns those who take advantage of them: 'If you spend yourselves on behalf of the hungry and satisfy the needs of the oppressed, then your light will arise in the darkness'.[15] There are many references like these that present an unmistakable sight of God's heart moved into action for the vulnerable.

No wonder we find Jesus with children, widows, sick, the dying or dead and with those who the religious groups looked down on—the sinners. His startling exposure of the judgment seat in heaven grips our attention and fills our thoughts with those who truly are His own people.[16] God's people, there at the judgement seat in Matthew 25, have the very same heart as His. They have such concern that it drives them quietly to serve the most vulnerable in their community, 'the least'. The amazing revelation here is that the King of heaven has His unique measure of their work. What they have done for 'the least' they actually, unknowingly have been doing it to the King and for the King.

How do we, as God's own people, see the vulnerable? Do I see them as the Lord sees them? Do I feel as He feels? These are vital questions. They lead us to decide how we take up the Lord's 'mission baton' in terms of what we do in practice and then how we will give an account to Him in eternity. The bottom line for me is this: does our church cater for those like Alice? Do we give as much priority to the marginalised as to those who appear not to be? Am I a trainee hero with the heart attitude of a slave? This is what Jesus wants us to grasp, alongside prayer, before any other church activity.[17]

Chapter 24

A Glimpse into the future

'Not because of who I am, but because of what You've done. Not because of what I've done, but because of who You are.'

Mark Hall, *Casting Crowns*

If you are a survivor, how are you after reading this book? I hope you are not full of negatives, because it is not always going to be like this. On our worst days we always have something to look forward to. 'Heaven is wonderful place, full of glory and grace' is a song we were taught at a family gathering by a young man engaged to our eldest daughter.

I have been convinced for many years that the least noticeable, behind-the-scenes saints will be the ones with the greatest honours and most significant jobs in heaven. Those who we do not hear very much about but who suffer quietly and think of themselves to be insignificant, weak, less honourable and unpresentable. It is these, who have come though suffering from the enemy of God's people, who are close to the throne of God. These are the ones who show us Jesus, His way and heaven.

We have this certainty as our unshakable hope and know that we are going to see for ourselves when Satan, the source of all our pain, will be 'hurled down'.[1] In heaven there are no break in's, there is no abuse or sexual exploitation, and our new bodies will not deteriorate. We will not even know what hunger, thirst or pain is. God our Father, himself will stoop down and wipe every tear from our eye.[2] It will be the end of it all.

But best by far, will be seeing the One who has suffered for us. So intense and complete will be Jesus' presence right in front of us, that, surely, everything of our past will become a far distant and faint memory; if we are able to remember it at all. 'The Lamb at the centre of the throne will be their shepherd; he will lead them to springs of living water.'[3] The shepherding care we have known now, will have been an introduction to his glorious protection and provision; we are now thoroughly refreshed with his direct presence. Jesus promised his disciples this: 'I am going to prepare a place for you. I will come back and take you to be with me that you also may be where I am'.[4]

If I don't see you before—I hope to see you there!

Before you go—are you a Christian?

You may have read this book and wondered, 'What does it mean to become a Christian?' This may well be because the Lord is getting your attention so that you follow him. I would encourage you to do three things. Each one is really a prayer, which simply is a conversation with God. You don't need it to be full of all the right sounding words. Just say to him what is on your heart.

- Ask the Lord to help you to really trust him to rescue you. Remember the Lord Jesus has done it all when he died in our place on the cross. He is the sacrifice for our sins; which means that God can now fully accept us because his anger against our sin has been put on Christ and not on us.[5] It is important that you give up trying to get God to accept you by doing things for him or by punishing yourself. You will never be good enough for God, or be able to do enough to please him. Remember, Jesus has done it all in our place and on our behalf. Jesus, alone makes us good by giving us his goodness as we trust in his cross and resurrection.
- Ask the Lord to forgive you for all that you have done (not for what someone else has done to you; that is not your responsibility). We need to tell him that he is right when he says that all of us: 'have sinned and fall short of the glory of God'.[6] God calls us to repent. That means to be genuinely sorry and turn away from our past to walk in a new direction with God. Thomas Watson, the Puritan preacher, wrote, 'Repentance and faith are both humbling graces; by repentance a man abhors himself, by faith he goes out of himself'.[7] He turns away from his own attempts to repay God and depends on what Jesus has done.
- Ask the Lord to show you a community of Christians who will walk with you. Our Father God does not expect us to walk alone. He brings His family together so that His children can be there for one another and learn together how to grow more like Jesus. Pray for a church who love the *word* of God (where truth is lovingly applied

to your life); who love to *witness* (loving the broken, the world and making disciples); who love to *worship* God (with an ardent love for God, a heart after Christ); who understand *wrestling* in prayer, and of great importance, who practice *welfare* (they have a genuine heart for one another and those outside the church).

'To him who is able to keep you from stumbling
and to present you before his glorious presence without fault and with great joy—
to the only God our Saviour be glory, majesty, power and authority,
through Jesus Christ our Lord, before all ages, now and for evermore!
Amen.'[8]

Epilogue

I have just come off the phone. Another unexpected turn of events. The police have been keeping me informed of the progress of the case against one of my perpetrators. He has just been sentenced to two years in prison.

He is now 81 years old and pleaded guilty to four indecent assaults on two other boys. He has been put on the sex offenders' register for 10 years. Sue and I were going to be called as witnesses but because he pleaded guilty it did not go to trial. It is standard procedure to serve half of the sentence so he will be in prison for one year.

He was one of the men who physically abused me. One of the men who sexually abused me died recently. There is a case being considered against the other teacher who sexually abused me.

There it is. Out of the four men who abused me, two are now dead, one is in prison and the other is being considered for trial. But when I began this process of dealing with the past I didn't expect any of these things to happen. The journey continues with much that is unexpected.

To sit down with a senior member of the clergy at the Cathedral and be heard was a great blessing. I spent a couple of hours with the Dean and a lady responsible for safe guarding and was then able to walk around the Cathedral and stand where I had sung to my Father in heaven. Up until then it was difficult to visit any Cathedral as it bought back so many upsetting memories. This was a worthwhile visit.

The police involvement in pursuing the men who are alive brings a sense of closure. God is just and faithful. He takes up our case. There is a great solace in seeing the loose ends tied up.

God's justice is ultimate and for decades I have left these four men in His hands. If they came to a point of truly repenting and even apologising to their victims that would give me great joy. But that too must be left in God's hands.

One step I have taken, in response to these developments, is to write a letter to my perpetrators. I have found this helpful as it draws a line under the place I have come to. It seems a fitting conclusion to all that the Lord has done. If this is not a good place for you to finish please turn back to Chapter 24 and read the first four paragraphs and finish with heaven! May all the glory go to God.

Epilogue

Dear perpetrator,

I am writing this letter not to retaliate but because I think it will help both of us.

It has been more than fifty years since you last saw me but I think about you often. I want you to know that what you did to me while I was at school has radically affected me. The abuse has injured my emotions and my thinking. Those minutes of pleasure for you have cost me a lifetime of pain. It is a kind of pain that is difficult for those who are not survivors to understand.

For many years after leaving boarding school I lacked confidence and all too often saw others as living in a much higher league to me. Anxiety, fear, insomnia, abandonment, anger, isolation, hopelessness and depression, are some of the things that I learnt to live with. Struggling with these symptoms of P.T.S.D. (Post Traumatic Stress Disorder) almost wrecked our marriage and brought me to the brink of suicide on many occasions. There were times when I misused drugs and alcohol to self-medicate the monster inside me.

Thankfully over the last few years, with the help of friends, counsellors and of course God my Father, I have managed to replace the monster. These things are now in the past. But I wanted to say this to you. By your selfish actions you took away an irreplaceable part of my life. You might have thought that you were loving, but love does not destroy another person.

But at least working through the trauma has driven me into the arms of Jesus. Your actions have also brought out a fight in me for a restoration in other survivors. The life change that victims and survivors deserve. I have gained so much while fighting to restore what the abuse had destroyed in me, that there is much for others to benefit from.

I don't know if you read your Bible but I can say what Joseph said to his brothers in Egypt: 'You intended to harm me, but God intended it for good to accomplish what is now being done, the saving of many lives" (Genesis 50:20). It gives me great comfort to know that all that I have suffered will be of some benefit to others, perhaps many others. Saving their marriage, cutting short their pain or drawing them into the arms of our loving heavenly Father.

Two of my perpetrators are already dead. As you are one of the remaining two, I dearly hope that before you die, you have an opportunity to come to terms with what you have done from God's perspective. This is the most important thing of all—to die knowing that Jesus has taken away all our sin because we have trusted Him to do it and to have inside us His life which will never die. May God, our mighty loving Father, do this for you if He hasn't already.

Most sincerely,
Robert

<table>
<tr><th colspan="2">THE REAL KING DAVID.
THE FOLLOWING VERSES ARE ALL FROM THE PSALMS.</th></tr>
<tr><th>DAVID'S EXPERIENCE</th><th>DAVID'S RESPONSE</th></tr>
<tr><td>Deeply troubled and Desperate
» 'My soul is in anguish. How long, O Lord, how long?'
» 'I am worn out from groaning, all night long I flood my bed with weeping and drench my couch with tears' (6:3,6)</td><td>» 'My shield is God Most High'
» 'I will give thanks to the Lord because of his righteousness and will sing praise to the name of the Lord Most High.' (7:10,17)
» 'The Lord is a refuge for the oppressed, a stronghold in times of trouble.' (9:9)</td></tr>
<tr><td>Deserted and vulnerable to evil men
» 'Help, Lord, for no one is faithful any more; those who are loyal have vanished from the human race.'
» '… the wicked who freely strut about when what is vile is honoured by the human race' (12:1,8)</td><td>» 'Because the poor are plundered and the needy groan, I will now arise,' says the Lord. 'I will protect them from those who malign them.'
» 'You, Lord, will keep the needy safe and will protect us for ever from the wicked,' (12:5,7)</td></tr>
<tr><td></td><td>» 'Keep me safe, my God for in you I take refuge. I keep my eyes always on the Lord. With him at my right hand, I shall not be shaken. Therefore my heart is glad and my tongue rejoices; my body also will rest secure ..' (16:1,8,9, whole Psalm)</td></tr>
</table>

Driven to the point of Death » 'The chords of death entangled me; the torrents of destruction **overwhelmed me.**' (18:4)	» 'I love you, Lord my strength. The Lord is my rock, my fortress and my deliverer; my God is my rock, in whom I take refuge ...' » 'He brought me out into a secure place; he rescued me because he delighted in me.' (18:1,2,19)
Isolated and alone » 'My God, my God why have you forsaken me? Why are you so far from saving me, so far from my cries of anguish? My God, I cry out by day, **but you do not answer,** by night, but I find no rest.' (22:1-2) **Self loathing, Rejected and mocked by others** » 'But I am **a worm and not a man,** scorned by eve-ryone and despised by the people. All who see me mock me; they hurl insults, shaking their heads.' (22:6-7)	» 'Yet you are enthroned as the Holy One; you are the One Israel praises.' (22:3) » 'Yet you brought me out of the womb; you made me trust in you, even at my mother's breast. From birth I was cast on you; from my mother's womb you have been my God.' (9-10) » 'Some trust in chariots and some in horses, but we trust in the name of the Lord our God.' (20:7)
Overcome by emotional pain that has aged him and makes him weak and ill » 'My life is **consumed by anguish** and my years by groaning; **my strength fails** because of my afflic-tion, and my bones grow weak.' (31:10, see 9)	» 'BUT I trust in you, Lord; I say, 'You are **my** God.' My times are in your hands; **deliver me** from my enemies and from those who pursue me. Let your light shine on your servant; **save me** in your unfailing love.' (31:14-17)
Worn out by own failings » 'My heart pounds, **my strength fails me; even the light has gone** from my eyes.' (38:10)	» 'Lord, **do not forsake me;** do not be far from me, my God. **Come quickly** to help me, **my** Lord and **my** Saviour.' (38:21-22)

Overwhelmed & Severely Distressed » 'For troubles without number surround me; my sins have overtaken me, and I cannot see. They are more than the hairs head and **my heart fails me.**' (40:12)	» 'I waited patiently for the Lord; **he** turned to me and heard my cry. **He** lifted me out of the slimy pit.. **he** set my feet on a rock… **He** put a new song in my mouth, a hymn of praise to our God. ..Blessed is the one who trusts in the Lord.' » 'But as for me, I am poor and needy; may the Lord think of me. **You are my help and my deliverer; you are my God, do not delay.**' (40:1-4,17)
Grieving & Depressed » '**My tears have been my food** day and night..' 'Why, my soul, are you downcast? Why so dis-turbed within me?' » 'My soul is **downcast** within me…' » 'My bones suffer mortal **agony** …' » 'Why, my soul, are you downcast? Why so dis-turbed within me?' (42:3,5,6,10,11)	» '**Put your hope in God,** for I will yet praise him, **my** Saviour and **my** God.' » 'By day the Lord directs his love, at night his song is with me – a prayer to the God of my life.' » 'Put your hope in God, for I will yet praise him, **my** Saviour and **my** God.' (42:5,8,11 + 46:1—whole)
Broken by his sin » 'My sacrifice, O God, is **a broken spirit; a broken and contrite heart,** you, God, will not despise.' (51:17)	
Distressed in fear and overwhelmed » 'My heart is in **anguish** within me; the terrors of death have fallen on me. Fear and trembling have beset me; horror has overwhelmed me.' (55:4-5)	» '**Cast your cares on the Lord** and he will sustain you; he will never let the righteous be shaken.' (55:22)

Broken, Helpless, Unstable & Alone	
» 'Save me, O God, for the waters have come up to my neck. **I sink** in the miry depths, where there is no foothold. I have come into the deep waters; **the floods engulf me.** I am **worn out** calling for help; my throat is parched. My eyes fail, looking for my God.' » 'Scorn has broken my heart and has left me **helpless**; I looked for sympathy, but there was **none**, for comforters, but **I found none.**' (69:1-3,20)	» 'BUT I **pray** to you, O Lord; » **Rescue** me from the mire, do not let me sink; deliver me from those who hate me, from the deep waters. » **Answer** me, O Lord, out of the goodness of your love; in your great mercy turn to me … » **Come near** and **rescue me; deliver me** because of my foes.' (69:13-18)
Utter failure » 'My flesh and my heart may fail;	» '**but God is the strength of my heart** and my por-tion for ever.' (73:26)
	» 'My heart, O God, **is steadfast;** I will sing and make music with **all** my soul. Awake, harp and lyre! I will awaken the dawn. I will **praise you**, O Lord, among the nations; I will **sing of you** among the peoples. For great is **your love,** higher than the heavens; **your faithfulness** reaches to the skies. Be exalted, O God, above the heavens, and let **your glory** be over all the earth.' 108:1-5

Appendix 2

WHEN WORKING WITH TRAUMA SURVIVORS **Developed from the work of Betsy de Thierry**			
Things that are invaluable	Things to provide	Things to avoid	Things to remember
Unshockable, unconditional love Total acceptance as an equal & a Non-judgemental attitude Hope and genuine en-couragement (small steps are significant steps) A firm belief that God brings about trans-formative change by the Spirit through His Word and serious prayer	Safety Regularity Consistency Reliability Education Genuine encouragement Support Dealing with the here and now before the then and there Symptom reduction and stabilisation Hope	Manipulation or Control Re-traumatising Total silence Looking shocked Dissociating Being volatile, aggressive Staying overwhelmed without passing through Negativity or saying things you do not mean Putting damaging thoughts into minds e.g. behave, be healed or get over it/forget it	You are not going to fix them. You are just facilitating the healing of the brainstem, the soul and the birth of a new person Survivors are survivors because they are brilliant at building self-protecting mechanisms The vast majority are not possessed but they are not in control of their symptoms Survivors have learnt to be acutely perceptive. Prayer, humility and genuine love are therefore essentials

Martin Luther's Poem

'Feelings come and feelings go,
And feelings are deceiving;
My warrant is the Word of God,
Naught else is worth believing.

Though all my heart should feel condemned
For want of some sweet token,
There is One greater than my heart
Whose Word cannot be broken.

I'll trust in God's unchanging Word
Till soul and body sever,
For, though all things shall pass away,
HIS WORD SHALL STAND FOR EVER!'[1]

Endnotes

CHAPTER 1

1 Judith Herman MD, *Trauma and Recovery: The Aftermath of Violence—From Domestic Abuse to Political Terror* (Basic Books, New York, 1992).

CHAPTER 2

1 Maxine Hancock & Karen Burton Mains, *Child Sexual Abuse: A Hope for Healing*, (Highland Books, Godalming, 1990), p.59.

2 'Working Together to Safeguard Children 2010' (1.33–1.36) referred to in NSPCC *Inform, Child Protection Fact Sheet: The definitions and signs of child abuse*, 2010', p.1.

3 Judith Herman, *Trauma and Recovery*, p.57.

4 'Purging and vomiting, compulsive sexual behaviour… the use of psychoactive drugs become the vehicles by which abused children attempt to regulate their internal emotional states.' Judith Herman, *Trauma and Recovery*, p.109.

5 'People who suffer PTSD (Post Traumatic Stress Disorder) often relive the experience through nightmares, flashbacks, have difficulty in sleeping and feel detached or estranged, and these symptoms can be severe enough and long enough to significantly impair the persons daily life'. Betsy De Thierry Seminar on 'Child Trauma and Dissociation'—Bristol, February 2013.

6 The National Child Traumatic Stress Network. 'Classically PTSD is a biphasic disorder with alternating phase of intrusion (feeling too much) and numbing (feeling too little) accompanied by hyperarousal and/or hypoarousal symptoms (fight or flight responses). This biphasic response is the result of dissociation: traumatic events are distanced and dissociated from usual conscious awareness in the numbing phase, only to return in the intrusive phase.' J.A.Chu (1998).

7 John.8:31–32, 37.

CHAPTER 3

1 Mark 8:24

2 2 Samuel 18:5, 9–15

3 2 Samuel 18:33ff

4 Matthew 11:28

CHAPTER 4

1 John 8:31–36

2 2 Samuel 13:19

3 Psalm 31:10 or 40:12

4 Psalm 27:10 (KJV), cf. Hebrews 13:5–6

5 Joel 2:25

6 John 8:31,36

CHAPTER 5

1 Jeremiah 18:1–6

2 Psalm 139:14

3 Psalm 139:13–18

4 Psa.139:16.

5 There is a mirror image of this in Ephesians 2:10, 'For we are God's workmanship, created in Christ Jesus to

do good works, which God prepared in advance for us to do.'

6 Ephesians 1:5

7 Exodus 3:5, Joshua 5:15

8 Ephesians 5:27

CHAPTER 6

1 See verses 1 Corinthians 6:9–10, Paul writes of the sexually immoral, idolaters, adulterers, male prostitutes, homosexual offenders, thieves, greedy, drunkards, etc, and then adds in v 11: 'But you were washed, you were sanctified, you were justified in the name of the Lord Jesus Christ and by the Spirit of our God.'

2 "There is widespread belief in a 'cycle' of child sexual abuse, but little empirical evidence for this belief …" http://bjp.rcpsych.org/content/179/6/482. Twenty-six of the 224 sex abuse victims (12%) later committed sexual offences, and in almost all cases their victims were also children. Roughly one in 10 male victims of child sex abuse in a U.K. study later went on to abuse children as adults. But the risk was far greater for sexually victimised children who came from severely dysfunctional families. Family history of violence, sexual abuse by a female, maternal neglect, and lack of supervision were all associated with a threefold-increased risk that the abused would become an abuser. The study is reported in the Feb. 8, 2003 issue of *The Lancet* by Bentovim and colleagues from London's Institute of Child Health.

CHAPTER 7

1 Warren W. Wiersbe, *Walking with the Giants,* (Baker Book House, Grand Rapids, Michigan, 1976) p.15

CHAPTER 8

1 Matthew 11:28

2 See also 2Corinthians 4:10

3 2 Corinthians 12:7ff

4 Colossians 1:22

CHAPTER 9

1 Judith Herman, *Trauma and Recovery: The Aftermath of Violence—From Domestic Abuse to Political Terror* (Basic Books, New York, 1992).

2 Gregory the Great gives this advice to preachers who rightly understand God's Word but do not speak it with humility to themselves: 'For indeed, he is a poor and unskilled physician who attempts to heal others but is not able to diagnose his own wounds. Therefore, those who do not speak the words of God with humility must be advised that when they apply medicine to the sick, they must first inspect the poison of their own infection, or else by attempting to heal others, they kill themselves. They ought to be advised that they take care so that their manner of speaking is consistent with the excellence of what is being said, and what they say with words is also preached by their actions. And let them hear what is written: "If anyone speaks, let him speak as the words of God" (1 Pet. 4:11)' Gregory the Great, *The Book of Pastoral Rule*, part III, chapter 24).

CHAPTER 10

1 Judith Herman, *Trauma and Recovery*, p.158
2 Psalm 139:1–4
3 Colossians.3:1–2
4 Psalm 139:7–12
5 Psalm 139:13–15
6 Psalm 139:17–18
7 Judith Herman, *Trauma and Recovery*, p.172
8 e.g. Psalms 32:7, 62:1–2, 91:1–2, 9–16, 125:1–2
9 Psalm 139:1, 23–24
10 2 Samuel 1:11–17; 12:16; 15:30; 18:33 and Nehemiah 1:3–4

CHAPTER 11

1 2 Samuel 18:33, Nehemiah 1:4
2 Genesis 50:1–4
3 Job 1:20; 1 Samuel 30:4; Matthew 2:18
4 John 11:35
5 Andreas Kostenberger, *ESV Study Bible*, 2007, (Crossway, Wheaton, Illinois).
6 Nehemiah 1:3–4
7 Nehemiah 1:4 to 2:5
8 2 Samuel 13:19
9 Nehemiah 1:4
10 Judith Herman, *Trauma and Recovery*, p.175
11 see Ephesians 3:16–21
12 see Nehemiah 1:11, 2:5,8
13 Nehemiah 2:11–12
14 Nehemiah 2:17–18
15 Matthew 5:4. Lenski points out that the verb presents to us a loud mourning like the lament for the dead or for a severe painful loss. This is akin to what the abused really do experience. The chief lament is sorrow for our own sin, with a grief or sorrow for 'the power of sin in the world as this inflicts blows, losses and pain on the godly.' Then Lenski adds, 'It includes every wrong done us, as well as every painful consequence of our own wrongdoing.' R.C.H.Lenski *The Interpretation of Matthew's Gospel* (The Wartburg Press, Minneapolis, 1943), p.186.
16 Nehemiah 1:4
17 Nehemiah 1:5–11
18 A grieving that is with hope, 'we do not want you … to grieve like the rest of men, who have no hope' 1Thessalonians 4:13. A hope that rests solidly in what Jesus has done in the past (at the cross) and will do in the future (at His return).
19 Joel 2:25–27 cf. Psalm 23:3
20 To have true fellowship we need to be in the light. 'if we walk in the light, as he is in the light, we have fellowship with one another, and the blood of Jesus his Son cleanses us from all sin' 1John 1:7

21 Matthew 27:46

22 Romans 5:3–5. John Murray shows how Paul describes here a circle of hope, through Suffering. Perseverance, Character to further Hope. In the centre of that circle I would put the love of God shed abroad in our hearts.

23 Galatians 5:22–23

24 'He heals the broken-hearted and binds up their wounds' Psalm 147:3.

CHAPTER 12

1 Lyndal Roper, *Martin Luther,* (Penguin, Random House UK, 2016), p.199.

2 Isaiah 35:8–10

3 Isaiah 35:10

4 Isaiah 61:7 'Instead of their shame my people will, receive a double portion and instead of disgrace they will rejoice in their inheritance …'

5 Lyndal Roper, *Martin Luther,* (Penguin, Random House UK, 2016), p.199. It is clear that at times Luther fought back. In Appendix 3 is a poem he wrote that I have found helpful.

6 Ephesians 6:14–16

7 This was developed from a course I heard about called the Lightning Process.

8 Jeremiah 29:11

9 Psalm 139:16

10 Romans 8:28

11 John 1:12, 1 John 3:1–2

12 Isaiah 1:18, Revelation 22:17

13 2 Corinthians 10:5

14 1 Corinthians 12:6,18,24

15 2 Corinthians 2:14–16

16 Philippians 4:8

17 Ephesians 6:12

18 Ephesians 6:10,13

19 Matthew 4:4

20 Hebrews 4:12

21 Thessalonians 5:18

CHAPTER 13

1 Matthew 5:23–24;18:15–17; John 13:34–35; 17:20–23; Acts 15:37–41; 2 Timothy 4:11; Galatians 5:25–6:2; Ephesians 2:14–16; 4:2–6; Philippians 4:2–3; Colossians 3:12–15; Philemon 15–17; Romans 12:10; 18–21; 16:17–18; 1 Peter 4:8; 2 Peter 1:7; 1 John 4:7ff; Genesis 27:41; 37:4–5; 50:19–21.

2 Philippians 4:2 'agree with each other' is the same word used in chapter 2:2 'like-minded'.

3 *ESV Study Bible*, (Crossway, 2008), p.2282.

4 Ephesians 4:29–32

5 Ephesians 5:1

6 Isaiah 40:31

7 Judith Herman, *Trauma and Recovery*, p.197

8 Colossians 3:3

9 1Corinthians 6:19

10 John17:22

11 James 1:2; Colossians 1:24

12 2 Corinthians 2:14–16, cf. 4:8–11

SECTION 3

1 Rachel Lloyd, *Girls Like Us—Fighting For A*

World Where Girls Are Not For Sale, Harper, 2011 p 267

CHAPTER 14

1 http://www.azquotes.com/quote/662842
2 Matthew 18:35.
3 Colossians 3:13.
4 Brian Edwards, *Grace—Amazing Grace* (Day One Publications, 2011), p.125.
5 Brian Edwards, *Grace—Amazing Grace*, (Day One Publications, Leominster 2011), p.140.
6 Luke 23:34.
7 Isaiah 38:17: 'You have put all my sins behind your back.' Jeremiah 31:34, 'I will forgive their wickedness and remember their sins no more.' Micah 7:18–19, 'who is a God like you who pardons sin and forgives … you will tread our sins under your foot and hurl all our iniquities into the depth of the sea.' Psalm 103:12, 'as far as the east is from the west, so far has he removed our transgressions from us.' See also 1 John 1:9, 'If we confess our sins, he is faithful and just and will forgive us our sins and purify us from all unrighteousness.'

CHAPTER 15

1 'You intended to harm me, but God intended it for good to accomplish what is now being done, the saving of many lives' Gen.50:20.
2 Psalm 6:3,6; 18:4; 22:1–2, 6–7; 31:10; 38:10; 40:12, or refer to the chart in Appendix 1 if you need to see more.
3 Psalm 42:3,5,7,10,11
4 1 Samuel 20:40–42
5 1 Samuel 27:7
6 Psalm 16:1,8,9
7 Psalm 40:1–4,17 and Psalm 90:14
8 Psalm 108:1–5
9 Psalm 34:8
10 Psalm 109:30–31
11 111:1ff
12 Luke 15:20–24

CHAPTER 16

1 Isaiah.61:1–3
2 Isaiah 61:3–4
3 Matthew 5:4

CHAPTER 17

1 Philippians 4:8
2 1 Corinthians 13 and 1 John 4
3 Luke 6:43–45
4 Proverbs 4:23
5 Hebrews 12:1–2
6 See also 1 Corinthians 10:13
7 Matthew 6:20–21
8 John 10:10
9 Zechariah 2:8
10 Psalm 57:1–4
11 Lamentations 3:31–33
12 Hebrews 12:15
13 Romans 8:28
14 Hebrews 12:25
15 1 Peter 5:8
16 Romans 2:14; 14:22; Acts 24:16; Hebrews

9:14;10:22

17 Isaiah 31:1

18 Psalm 119:25–32; Isaiah 30:15,16,18

19 1 Peter 2:21–23

20 Romans 5:8

21 Zechariah 3:3

22 2 Corinthians 5:21

23 Isaiah 30:18–26

24 Psalm 119.20; 42:1

25 Ephesians 2:8–10

26 Connie Neal, *Holding Onto Heaven While Your Husband Goes Through Hell*, (Word Publishing, Nashville, London, Vancouver, Melbourne, 1988). Stormie Omartian, *The Power of a Praying Wife*, (Kingsway Publication, Eastbourne, 1977). The Bible: Daniel's prayer in Daniel 9:3–19 and the Lord's prayer in Matthew 6:9–13.

27 Judith Herman, *Trauma and Recovery*, p.150

28 Z. Hereford, *Healthy Personal Boundaries & How to Establish Them,* http:// www.essentiallifeskills.net/personalboundaries.html

29 Ruth Robb, An extract from an internal communication, June 2015 for the charity Azalea

30 Romans 8:28; 2 Corinthians 5:7

31 Genesis 15:6

32 Ephesians 5:31–32

33 Mark 9:29 (*New King James Version*)

34 John 10:10

35 Romans 12:2

36 Joshua 1:9; Ephesians 6:10–18

37 2 Peter 2:21–23; Acts 17:9,10

38 Isaiah 61:1–4; Deuteronomy 7:21–22; 2 Chronicles 20:15ff

39 Ecclesiastes 4:12

CHAPTER 18

1 Jay E Adams, *The Christian Counsellor's Manual*, (Baker Book House, 1973) p.175.

2 1 Corinthians 6:19

3 Psalm 61:2

4 Romans 6:2–4

5 Romans 6:5–7,9 cf 11–14,18–23

6 Ephesians 4:22–24

7 Ephesians 4:22–23

8 Romans 12:2

9 Romans 8:6

CHAPTER 19

1 Isaiah 43:19

2 2 Corinthians 5:17, Philippians 3:13–15, Jeremiah 29:11

3 John 8:31–32, Romans 8:28

CHAPTER 20

1 Hancock & Mains, amid, p.73

2 Philippians 2:13

3 Philippians 4:8.

4 Judith Herman, *Trauma and Recovery*, p.195.

5 For example 1 Samuel 13:14, 16:7 and Genesis 50:20

6 Ezekiel 36:26; 2 Corinthians 5:17.

7 Titus 2:11–15 and 2 Corinthians 3:18.

8 Galatians 5:16–26.

Endnotes

9 2 Corinthians 5:17.

10 2 Corinthians 3:17.

11 John 8:36

12 Psalm 82:3-5.

13 Isaiah 40:31.

CHAPTER 21

1 https://www.goodreads.com/author/quotes/31779.Alejandro_Jodorowsky

2 Many attribute this to Sir Winston Churchill but there is little evidence that it is his. The origins of it point to a self-help counsellor named Douglas Bloch who wrote an article in 1990 entitled, 'If you're going through hell, don't stop' In the article he says to his interviewer, 'When someone says, 'I'm going through hell the best response is to tell them, 'Don't stop!' Bloch maintains. If we see that pain, grief and tough times are a process and that it will get better, we're less likely to get stuck in the hell.' Quote Investigator—Exploring the Origins of Quotations, http://quoteinvestigator.com/2014/09/14/keep-going/

3 Gerald Boerner has written about her and the movements she was involved with http://www.boerner.net/ jboerner/?p=7769

4 Mark Hall and Matthew West, 'Thrive'—Casting Crowns, track 1, 2013, (Sony, ATV Tree Publishing)

5 Luke 15:11–32

6 Luke 15:22–24

7 Romans 12:2

8 Revelation 3:8

9 Revelation 3:7

10 Philippians 3:13 cf. 1Thessalonians 5:23–24

11 I have a poster in front of my desk with these three scriptures on it (Revelation 3:8–10; 1 Corinthians 15:58 and 2 Corinthians 1:8–11) and the statement 'I can do this because Jesus says so and he says he will do it with me.'

12 1 Peter 1:13

13 Revelation 3:8

CHAPTER 22

1 Bowley, Mary Frances, *The White Umbrella: Walking with Survivors of Sex Trafficking*, (Moody Publishers, Chicago, 2012), p.193.

2 Galatians 6:1–2

3 Galatians 6:2 'the law of Christ' in its widest sense means all of His teachings but in a specific sense it refers to the law of love, to love one's neighbour as oneself.

4 Romans.3:22–23

5 Matthew 5:1–12

6 In Appendix 2 is a chart 'Working with Trauma Survivors' that lists suggestions of what to provide and things to avoid.

CHAPTER 23

1 John 4:35, 27

2 *Truth Magazine*,Vol. XLIV: 9, May 4, 2000, p.18

3 John 4:14

4 Luke 7:36–50

5 Isaiah 25:1,4
6 Isaiah 58:10
7 Psalm 41:1–3
8 Luke14:10,13
9 Luke 7:36–50
10 Acts 6:1–6
11 Matthew 25:31–46
12 Ephesians 6:10–18
13 Matthew 28:19–20
14 Deuteronomy10:18
15 Isaiah 58:10
16 Matthew 25:31–46
17 See Mark 9:35–36 cf. Amos 5:21–24

CHAPTER 24

1 Revelation 12:7–9
2 Revelation 7:16–17
3 Revelation 7:17
4 John 14:2–3
5 Romans 3:21–25
6 Romans 3:23
7 Thomas Watson, *Body of Divinity* (Baker Book House, Michigan, 1979) p.150
8 Jude 24–25

APPENDIX 3

1 John R. Rice (Compiled & Edited by), *742 Heart-Warming Poems* (Sword of the Lord Publishers,1964) p 18

Reference list

Mary Frances Bowley, *The White Umbrella: Walking with Survivors of Sex Trafficking* (Moody Publishers, Chicago, 2012)

Heather Churchill & Wendy Bray, *Insight into Helping Survivors of Childhood Sexual Abuse* (CPR, 2012)

Barbara Glasson, *A Spirituality of Survival: Enabling a Response to Trauma & Abuse* (Continuum, 2009)

Judith Herman MD, *Trauma and Recovery: The Aftermath of Violence – from Domestic Abuse to Political Terror'* (Basic Books, New York, 1992).

Maxine Hancock and Karen Burton Mains, *Child Sexual Abuse: A Hope for Healing* (Highland Books, 1987)

Rachel Lloyd, *Girls Like Us: A Memoir—Fighting for a World Where Girls are Not for Sale* (Harper Perennial, 2011)

Mez McConnell, *Is there Anybody Out There? A Journey from Despair to Hope* (Christian Focus Pub., 2006)

Chris Williams, Paul Richards and Ingrid Whitton, *I'm not Supposed to Feel Like This: A Christian Self-help Approach to Depression and Anxiety* (Hodder & Stoughton, 2002)

Brian Edwards, *Grace—Amazing Grace: Unpacking the Reality of God's Incredible Love* (Day One Publications, Leominster, 2011)

Stuart Olyott, *Known & Felt: A Missing Note In Today's Christianity* (Evangelical Movement of Wales, 2014)

CPR—Offering Life Support to Prisoners

PO Box 61685 | London | SE9 9BL

Website: www.cprministries.org.uk

Email: admin@cprministries.org.uk

Tel: 07749373185

The vision of CPR is to see prisoners' lives transformed, their relationships restored and their communities rebuilt as they understand the good news of Jesus Christ.

CPR partners with prison chaplains and churches, to inspire prisoners with the Good News of Jesus Christ through personal and practical resourcing—equipping them biblically to enjoy the Christian hope for themselves.

COURAGEOUS EXCHANGE PROGRAMME

(Transformation from Child Abuse & Addiction)

HOPE | 68 New Bedford Road | Luton LU2 7NT

Website: www.courageous.online

Email: robert.courageous@gmail.com

The Courageous Exchange Programme is an interactive journey of transformation. Bible based group work, coaching and individual exercises reinforce healthy and fulfilling relationships. Each module involves self-monitoring, live examples, reviews, and mutual support. The interactive course material and personal mentoring enables a journey away from the effects of child abuse and sexual addiction.

Stop It Now—Together new can prevent Child Sexual Abuse

www.stopitnow.org.uk

Journey UK—Created For Relationships

www.journey-uk.org

Beyond The Streets—Working to End Sexual Exploitation

www.beyondthestreets.org.uk

Courageous Exchange—Transformation from Child Abuse & Addiction

www.courageous.online

Also available

Workbook 2: Breaking the Silence on Child Abuse—A Study

BY ROBERT LIGHTOWLER

This is a workbook that can be used with Robert Stevens's *Breaking the Silence on Child Abuse*.

Group work is a way forward for some, while others prefer to look into these things by themselves. The workbook is designed to help progress on a journey of recovery.

Workbook 1: Foundations—A Study

BY ROBERT LIGHTOWLER